T0199146

LEADING BUSINESS BEYOND PROFIT

A PRACTICAL GUIDE TO LEADING A BUSINESS TO PROFIT AND SIGNIFICANCE

Michiel Frederick Coetzer, Ph.D

WESTBOW
P R E S S®
A DIVISION OF THOMAS NELSON
& ZONDERVAN

WestBow Press books may be ordered through booksellers or by contacting:

WestBow Press
A Division of Thomas Nelson & Zondervan
1663 Liberty Drive
Bloomington, IN 47403
www.westbowpress.com
1 (866) 928-1240

ISBN: 978-1-9736-3849-0 (sc)
ISBN: 978-1-9736-3850-6 (hc)
ISBN: 978-1-9736-3848-3 (e)

Library of Congress Control Number: 2018914439

Print information available on the last page.

WestBow Press rev. date: 12/27/2018

Contents

Author declaration

The content of this book is a consolidation and extension of the following original published works:

- Coetzer, M. F., Bussin, M., & Geldenhuys, M. (2017). The functions of a servant leader. *Administrative Sciences, 7*(5), 1-32. doi:10.3390/admsci7010005.
- Coetzer, M. F. (2018). *The impact of a servant leadership intervention on work engagement and burnout* (Doctoral dissertation). University of Johannesburg, Johannesburg, South Africa.
- Coetzer, M. F. (2018). A conceptual framework to operationalise servant leadership within an organisation. In D. Van Dierendonck and K. Patterson (Eds.), *Practicing Servant Leadership: Developments in Implementation*. London: Palgrave Macmillan.

CHAPTER 1
THE LEADERSHIP CRISIS

Imagine a world without poverty, crime, corruption, fraud, stress, abuse, war, poor service delivery, economic problems, unemployment, and physical or mental ill health. Imagine a world where people care for each other, respect each other, and help each other. Imagine a world where everyone has a meaningful job, adequate education, exceptional healthcare, a loving family life, restful vacations, a cozy home, and a safe environment. Imagine people enjoying their work and experiencing true joy, freedom, peace, and fulfillment while working. Imagine leaders who serve their people, organizations, and societies with integrity, love, and purpose, to create a better world for all. Imagine a world where organizations serve their customers and society with products and services that create sustainable value and are good, healthy, and beneficial. Imagine a world where business is based on love and purpose, instead of fear and greed. Imagine what the world would look like when people serve each other with their gifts, time, and talents. Imagine a world where children spend more time with their parents than with caretakers. Imagine a world where children play caring and kind games. Imagine a world where marriage is sacred and people experience happiness and fulfillment in their relationships. Imagine a world where murder and immorality are not entertainment, exploitation is not selling, and accumulation is not success. Imagine a world without depression, anxiety, fear, burnout, cancer, diabetes, or cardiovascular disease. Imagine a world where people are healthy, eat nutritious food, are fit, have a healthy sense of self-worth, and feel valued, accepted, and loved. Imagine a world where people are patient, loving, kind, caring, forgiving, and generous. Imagine how people would feel, think, and behave in such a world.

Sadly, the world we live in today is characterized by fraud, corruption, stress-related ill health, poverty, economic problems, and political instability. For example, PricewaterhouseCoopers (2018) reported that 49% of organizations globally experience economic crime. Their report also indicates that global economic crime significantly increased after 2016. Another global problem is stress-related ill health. The World Health Organization (2015) revealed that stress-related illnesses such as cardiovascular disease, cancer, chronic respiratory diseases, and diabetes are the biggest threat to human existence, and are responsible for approximately 70% of human deaths worldwide. A third social challenge is poverty. The World Bank reported that approximately 783 million people are still living in extreme poverty, although much progress has been made to decrease poverty in recent years (Lakner, Azevedo, Mahler, & Prydz 2018). In the last decade, the world also experienced a range of economic problems, such as the global financial crisis of 2008 and 2009, the European debt crisis of 2010 and 2011, and the global community price readjustments of 2014 to 2016 (United Nations 2018). Political instability has also taken its toll, not only in the last century, but across the history of human existence. World War II, for example, claimed more than 50 million human lives in just six years (from 1939 to 1945). According to the *New York Times*, humans have been at complete peace for only 8% of recorded history, and that approximately 1 billion people have died due to political instability (Hedges 2003). These are just a few examples of the global challenges in the last decade or century, and do not even include the world's current environmental problems and the depletion of natural resources.

Although one can see glimpses of the ideal in the current world, a lot of work is still to be done to create and sustain a better world for all. We have the opportunity and the responsibility to create and sustain a better world for current and future generations, because we have more knowledge, technology, wisdom, and historic information at our disposal than any other generation before us. There is thus no excuse anymore for negligent behavior.

Business seems to be the perfect mechanism to create a constructive and sustainable world, as it resides at the center of society. Without business, people will not have jobs, governments will not have taxes, society will not have schools, hospitals, and infrastructure, and churches and charities will not receive tithes and donations. Business has the potential to promote the wealth, wellbeing, and welfare of all people and to create a sustainable society for current and future generations. However, before business can create and sustain a long-lasting, positive legacy in society, it is important to understand its current limitations and challenges. One of the current limitations to creating and sustaining a better world for all is the manipulation of capitalism.

Initially, capitalism was designed to create value for people and society, and history shows the benefits of this economic system. Mackey and Sisodia (2014) highlighted a few examples of how capitalism has served people and society in the past, namely:

- *Decreased poverty:* About 85% of the world's population lived in extreme poverty approximately 200 years ago. In recent years, the rate decreased to 11%. The percentage of undernourished people also dropped, from 26% to 13%, over the last 40 years.
- *Increased average income per capita:* The average income per capita globally increased by 1 000% since 1800.
- *Increased literacy levels:* From a world of almost complete illiteracy, about 84% of adults can now read.
- *Increased political stability:* With the growth of economic freedom, 53% of people now live in countries with democratic governments, compared to 0% just 120 years ago.
- *Increased life expectancy:* The average life expectancy increased from 30 years (200 years ago) to 68 years, due to the advancements in medical technology, living standards, and nutrition, and a decrease in war activity.

However, in recent years, people and businesses have started to manipulate capitalism to serve selfish needs, without considering the larger impact on people, society, and the environment. Current misuses of capitalism include corporate dictatorship, customer exploitation, labor exploitation, and environmental exploitation.

1.1 Corporate dictatorship

Corporate dictatorship refers to the misaligned distribution of wealth and power to a small proportion of the human population or companies, which then leaves the majority of people (and other companies) exploited. This small proportion of elite and powerful organizations or people then have major power and influence over political affairs, activities, and legislation, and they use this power with utter disregard for human rights, democracy, and freedom. The problem with corporate dictatorship is that a few major organizations or people might abuse their power to bend legislation to serve their own needs, without considering the interests and needs of all stakeholders, including other individuals, society, and the environment. Another problem with corporate dictatorship is that a few major corporations or a small proportion of people have the ability to manipulate or exploit the market to sell more products, without considering the holistic impact, which may result in a recession. These major organizations are often "too big to fail" or "too big to jail". When these organizations fail, it requires government intervention to save society from devastation.

Corporate dictatorship is driven by the greediness of humankind. People and society have a dire need for more altruistic leaders and businesses that serve the true needs of people, society, and the environment, instead of greedy leaders who serve only their own selfish need to accumulate more power and status, to the detriment of others. Business should thus be driven by serving a need and not by satisfying a greed.

1.2 Customer exploitation

The second misuse of capitalism is customer exploitation. Customer exploitation refers to any form of customer abuse or manipulation. A few examples of customer exploitation are: creating false needs, producing destructive products and services, intentional market abuse, persuasive marketing campaigns, and poor after-sale service.

1.2.1 Creating false needs

Many of the products and services people use today are not things they really need. Companies often create false needs by promoting their products or services in such a way that consumers believe they need it. Creating these false needs is driven by greed, not the desire to serve the real needs of people and society. Some business schools even teach the idea of creating a need instead of identifying and serving a need. This is nothing less than exploitation.

An example of creating a false need is the release of a new motor vehicle without any real additional value compared to the model being replaced. A vehicle manufacturer may decide to release a new version of a motor vehicle of which the design was slightly changed, but the value to the consumer remains more or less the same. These manufacturers then sell the new product at a higher price and bargain on the greediness of humankind to buy the new version. Some people will sell their older, paid-off vehicles that are still in good working condition to buy the newer version, in the process acquiring additional debt. This consumer does not receive any real additional value or benefit, but the company makes more profit. This is not to the benefit of people or society. Living debt-free is preferable to serving debt, but most companies encourage debt in order to sell more products, without considering what is truly best for the consumer.

People buy things they do not need and for the wrong reasons, such as to ease their dissatisfaction with life, enhance their self-worth and pride and boost their ego or status. Many companies capitalize on these weaknesses by cleverly designing products and services to aggravate these feelings of inadequacy, and deploy persuasive marketing techniques to get people to buy things they do not really need. Two scenarios can be used to illustrate this point. The first scenario is the development of artificial intelligence. Currently, a lot of effort, time, and money is spent on developing robots that people do not really need and that might even be destructive to the sustainability of humankind in the future. The name of this industry says it all — artificial, which means 'false'. One could ask the question: What is the main reason for developing robots? In many instances, the intent for developing robots is to enhance productivity and to make more money. A second example is people using the same effort, time, and money to develop technology to purify seawater to resolve the issue of droughts in many countries. In this scenario, the intent is to serve a real need in society, namely the scarcity of water. The key principle is therefore the intent of the design and application. Organizations should design products and services to serve the real needs of people and society, instead of feeding on the greed of humankind.

1.2.2 Destructive products and services

Another form of customer exploitation is destructive products and services. Some companies misuse capitalism to design products and services that are not beneficial to people or society. An example of a destructive product is cigarettes. The main intent of a cigarette manufacturer is to accumulate money, which occurs to the detriment of addicted individuals. The addictiveness and negative consequences of smoking are well known, yet companies continue to manufacture cigarettes. These companies do not consider the welfare of their customers; their only aim is to exploit customers to make money.

Any product that is not truly and sustainably beneficial to customers can thus be classified as a destructive product. Organizations should aim to develop and promote products and services that are truly beneficial to customers, and refrain from offering products and services that are harmful or do not add value to people's lives and to society.

1.2.3 Intentional market abuse

A third form of customer exploitation is intentional market abuse. Market abuse refers to withholding or adding an important variable to a product or service that the investor or consumer of the product is not necessarily aware of, or to manipulate the demand or supply of a market to make more money. For example, a company might delay the release of new technology in an attempt to make more money over time. In this instance, the company will spread the release of the technology over a longer period, to sell more products. An example of such a product is computers. The release of this technology was delayed over time (and still is), to force customers to buy the next phase of the release. After a period, the previous release will become irrelevant, and the customer then has no choice but to buy the latest release. This is nothing less than manipulating the demand and supply of a market.

Another example is the release of video games. Often, video game manufacturers intentionally design a new release of a product in such a way that the previous games will not work on the newly released game console, forcing customers to buy the new product *and* new games. All the previous versions of the product will thus become obsolete over time. The intent with the new version of the product is thus to make more money, to the disadvantage of customers.

A third example of market abuse is when companies design a product to fail over time, to force customers to buy more of it in the future, or when a company intentionally adds a variable to its products to stimulate the usage thereof. For instance, a toothpaste manufacturer might decide to enlarge the tip of a toothpaste tube to ensure the consumer uses more of the product quicker, meaning that the consumer needs to buy more of the product sooner. These techniques and methods of market abuse are often unknown to the consumer, and such companies make no effort to communicate this authentically to customers before they buy the product.

1.2.4 *Persuasive marketing campaigns*

A fourth form of customer exploitation is persuasive marketing campaigns. Many advertising and marketing campaigns use immoral techniques to persuade people to buy products or services, *creating* a need instead of *serving* a need. Marketing and advertising are based on the so-called 'vulnerability stimuli' — playing on people's insecurities to trigger or create a false need. One example of such marketing is child-targeted advertisements. Children are less able than adults to control their impulses and apply self-control. Some companies target the vulnerability stimuli of children in their marketing campaigns. Another example of persuasive marketing is to use some form of sensual content when advertising products. Any form of marketing that entices a person into buying a product or service by triggering vulnerable stimuli is not promoting the common good of humankind, but is creating a society ruled by impulsiveness, thoughtlessness, and lack of self-control. Any product or service that needs persuasive marketing should be regarded with suspicion. A product or service that addresses the real needs of people and society does not need persuasive marketing; it will sell itself by virtue of the value it holds for users.

1.2.5   Poor after-sale service

A fifth form of customer exploitation is poor after-sale service. In some companies, the response time in the sales department is much shorter than in the customer-support department. For example, a customer phoning a provider to acquire a new Internet service will enjoy a much faster response time than the customer who has already bought the product and signed an annual subscription fee and now requires technical support. This clearly shows the company's main focus and intent. Such companies show their customers that their selfish intent of making more sales is more important than rendering valued services to their loyal customers.

If a company's main intent is to serve people and society with valuable products and services, the customer-support department will have a better response time than the sales department. Any company that sells a continuous product or service without offering any form of value-adding customer support, during and after the sale, is exploiting customers in an attempt to make more money, to the detriment of the customer. Companies should rather have the customer's best interests at heart, especially in its operating principles and practices. When good products are supported by exceptional after-sale service, loyal customers will become ambassadors of the company, and increased sales will become an automated response.

1.3 Labor exploitation

Another way that companies misuse capitalism is exploitation of the labor force. Most companies bargain on the excessive value that employees produce, beyond their own survival and personal needs, to make profit. Companies often abuse or stretch this excessive value in an attempt to make more money. For example, in a retrenchment process, a company might retrench some of its employees to lower turnover costs, in order to make more profit, and, in the process, allocate more work to the remaining employees, without paying them for the additional work. Companies do this knowing that there is always someone desperate enough to accept the excessive workload with lower pay. The employee threatened with retrenchment then has no choice but to compromise on his or her basic human needs, such as family time, rest, and work–life balance, to take up the extended role for the same pay. This is nothing less than labor exploitation.

The stress-related mental and physical illnesses evident in the world are proof of how organizations exploit employees. As mentioned before, stress-related non-communicable diseases were identified as the biggest threat to human existence, responsible for more than 70% of human deaths worldwide (World Health Organization 2015). Most of these diseases are enhanced or even caused by stress or burnout. This means that stress and burnout are a major threat to human existence. People who experience high levels of stress or are burnt out are also less energized, motivated, focused, and productive, resulting in poor employee- and organizational performance and, ultimately, poor economic growth. In an attempt to increase profits, companies initiate additional cost-cutting measures, such as retrenchments, that often result in higher levels of stress-related ill health and burnout of the remaining employees, which then affect the overall performance and productivity of employees negatively and reduce profits significantly. In an attempt to further reduce costs to make more profit, companies then initiate another retrenchment process and so the vicious cycle continues, until either the employee or the business fails.

The low employee engagement rates globally might further indicate how companies exploit employees. Work engagement is an individual state in which a person experiences high levels of energy, motivation, and focus while working (Bakker & Demerouti 2008). High work engagement is a state — not a choice, characteristic, or intrinsic variable. It is dependent on the work environment in the organization, in other words, the employees' experience of the job demands and job resources in the company (Bakker & Demerouti 2007). The individual state of work engagement can also vary over time.

According to Gallup (2013), only 13% of employees in the world experience high engagement in their work. This low rate of employee engagement is an indicator that most employees in the world are not energized, motivated, or engrossed while working, most probably due to excessive job demands (workload, mental load, and emotional load), and do not have the required job resources (Schaufeli & Bakker 2004). Job resources are organizational resources (physical resources, communication, remuneration), social resources (good supervisor- and colleague relationships), developmental resources (performance feedback, learning and development, self-perceived competence, and career path), and positional resources (person–job fit, role clarity, and job information) that an employee needs to buffer the negative effects of high job demands (Schaufeli 2015). Labor is thus exploited when high or extreme job demands are made of employees, without providing the necessary job resources.

Another, more serious, form of labor exploitation is modern slavery, which includes forced labor, human trafficking, debt bondage, descent-based slavery, and child labor. The International Labour Organization and Walk Free Foundation (2017) indicated that approximately 40 million people globally are victims of modern slavery, with the majority of forced labor (67%) evident in the private sector. The World Economic Forum also revealed that the total estimated profit generated from modern slavery is about $150 billion annually, of which $43 billion is from forced labor (Zweynert 2015). These statistics indicate that a lot is still required to free people from slavery.

Organizations that exploit people to make more profit do not consider the higher purpose or the holistic impact of business. Businesses need people to buy their products and services, and people need businesses to earn a living and to have money to buy products and services. The one cannot exist without the other. Business should therefore serve people and society by ensuring it creates sustainable value for customers and employees and creates jobs for people to earn a living. In return, businesses benefit from the wealth — purchasing power — of people and society. Responsible organizations therefore understand that labor exploitation is not useful, beneficial, or sustainable for business, people, or society.

1.4 Environmental exploitation

People, society, and businesses depend on natural and environmental resources to survive. Any business uses some form of environmental resource to produce a product or service, including minerals such as gold, copper, coal, iron ore, water, oil, oxygen, and land. Therefore, they cannot survive without natural or environmental resources. However, many organizations abuse these resources to make more profit, without considering the holistic impact of their actions.

Environmental exploitation can be defined as individuals or organizations abusing natural or environmental resources to achieve selfish objectives without considering the longitudinal impact thereof on the environment, the ecosystems, and future generations of humans, plants, or animals, and by not considering the sustainability of the resource (Nagtzaam 2009). Some examples of the consequences of environmental exploitation are: deforestation, desertification, water scarcity, extinction of species, forced migration, soil erosion, global warming, oil or mineral depletion, ozone depletion, and natural disasters.

An analogy can be used to illustrate the impact of environmental exploitation. Imagine a small village of people living in a forest. Every week, each family needs the wood of one tree to cook food and to keep themselves warm at night. However, none of these families planted another tree in their lifetime. A century later, the previous generation have all died leaving the forest without any trees for the next generation. This means that their children and grandchildren do not have any wood to cook food or to keep themselves warm at night. At this time, it is also too late for the next generation to plant trees to meet the weekly need of wood, as a tree takes five years to grow. The animals in the forest have also died, as they were dependent on the trees for food, leaving the next generation of people without food and skins to make clothes. The selfishness and irresponsibility of the previous generation therefore negatively impacted the survivability of the next generation.

The same principle applies in society and business. If people and organizations abuse environmental resources without considering the impact on its sustainability for future use, they cause the next generation to suffer. As the survival of any organization depends on the availability of natural and environmental resources to produce a product or service, it is imperative to protect and nurture those resources to sustain the survival of current and future societies and businesses.

1.5 The leadership crisis

The limitations to building the ideal world discussed above are not caused by the system (capitalism), but by the leaders using the system. The intent of application is what really matters. Self-serving leaders will use capitalism to accumulate more wealth and wellbeing to the detriment of others, society, and the environment, whereas servant-leaders will use capitalism to create sustainable wealth and wellbeing for multiple stakeholders, to the benefit of society and the environment.

Leadership theories have been researched for decades, and history has shown the positive and negative impact of different leadership practices. However, the negative consequences of ineffective leadership are evident everywhere: political instability, wars, poverty, fraud and corruption, manipulation of capitalism, modern slavery, environmental destruction, low employee engagement, low talent retention in organizations, poor organizational performance, and economic hardship. This is an indication that current leadership theories and practices are not effective in sustaining the world, now or in the future. These problems indicate a global leadership crisis that has never been resolved in the history of humankind.

Over the last century, companies have spent billions to develop leaders in organizations, and have used different training methods to cultivate new leaders in business and society. However, problems such as low work engagement and stress-related ill health remain evident in organizations, despite these development efforts. Some blame the ineffectiveness of the leadership development programs and suggest that the training methods should change. Others believe the world is changing too fast to equip leaders with the right competencies to lead, and that the world is therefore experiencing a leadership gap.

Maybe the problem is not the development program, learning method, or the rapidly changing world, but rather the leadership approach that is taught in the program. Many business schools focus on equipping leaders with the technical ability to run a business, but neglect to transform the heart of the leader, which is actually the most crucial part of effective leadership. As a result, there are many self-serving leaders in business and government who aim to accumulate more wealth, power, and status for themselves, to the detriment of other people, without leaving any form of positive legacy.

Leaders can have all the technical abilities, competencies, and economic know-how, but with the wrong leadership heart, these abilities will be used with the wrong intent, and will wreak destruction in the world. The devastating consequences of self-serving leadership are clearly evident in the history of humankind. The past and current problems in the world clearly indicate the desperate need for a more effective and sustainable leadership approach, namely servant leadership.

1.6 Difference between self-serving versus servant leadership

The main differentiator between self-serving and servant leadership is intent. Self-serving leaders lead from a motive or intent to achieve selfish goals to the detriment of others and society, whereas servant-leaders lead from a motive and intent to serve people, organizations, society, and the environment. Self-serving leaders have a 'get' mentality, while servant-leaders have a 'give' mentality. Self-serving leaders focus on accumulation, servant-leaders focus on collective positive impact. Self-serving leaders use practices such as fear, control, greed, and pressure to get results, and often abuse their power to accomplish selfish goals. Servant-leaders, on the other hand, use practices such as purpose, talent alignment, empowerment, and support to achieve goals that benefit multiple stakeholders, and use their leadership position to create sustainable positive change in business, people, society, and the environment. Self-serving leadership is characterized by selfishness, jealousy, greed, narcissism, manipulation, Machiavellianism, personalized charisma, a need for power, and psychopathy. These characteristics are driven by a heart of pride and fear. The characteristics of a servant-leader include courage, altruism, compassion, integrity, accountability, authenticity, humility, and the ability to listen, and originate from a heart of love and purpose.

A self-serving leader produces destructive outcomes for organizations and abuses organizational resources to serve selfish needs. For example, a self-serving leader might abuse the training budget of a company to attend expensive conferences or executive training courses for personal gain, and neglect to provide training opportunities to other employees in the organization to empower and support them to achieve personal and organizational goals. A self-serving leader will also limit the performance potential of an organization. For instance, a self-serving leader will hoard critical knowledge, information, or skills to remain in power. Employees then remain dependent on the leader to perform, which hinders organizational competence and performance. A self-serving leader, furthermore, exposes the organization to unethical and unlawful practices that put the organization at risk and damage its reputation. The corrupt behavior of one selfish leader can, in a day, destroy an organization's reputation that took decades to build.

Other destructive organizational outcomes that self-serving leaders produce are poor service delivery, poor product quality, low productivity, and unsustainable financial performance. For example, a self-serving leader might decrease the quality of a product by removing small parts in the manufacturing process, or retrench people in the after-sales department to reduce overheads. As a result, the customer receives reduced quality for the same price, and will not receive adequate support when the product fails. Customer trust in the company then decreases, which means that customers will not repurchase products from the company in the future or recommend the product to others. This will ultimately cause a decrease in sales.

Self-serving leaders not only produce negative outcomes for organizations, they also have a negative impact on people. People working under self-serving leaders experience more stress, leading to higher physical and psychological ill health. Self-serving leaders also cause higher employee turnover, increased absenteeism, and overall work- and life dissatisfaction. These destructive individual outcomes then negatively influence the employees' ability to perform.

In contrast, servant-leaders produce positive organizational and individual outcomes. For example, servant-leaders apply good stewardship and use organizational resources wisely to produce the best return on investment, to the benefit of multiple stakeholders (the customer, employee, shareholder, supplier, society, and the environment). Servant-leaders also continuously develop and empower employees to perform better, which leads to improved overall organizational competence and performance. Servant-leaders do business ethically, as they possess high levels of integrity, and they reduce organizational risks because they are accountable and good stewards.

Servant-leaders are also service-orientated; they serve customers, employees, shareholders, suppliers, society, and the environment to the best of their ability. In return, the organization benefits from more sales (due to repeat business and customer referrals), higher retention of employee talent, more capital investment by shareholders, better supplier relationships and partnerships, a supportive society, and a sustainable environment.

Servant-leaders not only serve. They also think, plan, and deliver. They instill a higher-purpose vision in the organization, to achieve collective benefits for people, society, and the environment. They also create a serving culture in the organization and empower employees to serve the customer and society, to ultimately achieve the higher-purpose vision. In this way, servant-leaders create a more sustainable world for all.

Servant-leaders also influence individuals positively. For example, servant-leaders serve the needs of employees by providing the required resources to employees to achieve individual and organizational goals. This enhances the employees' work engagement, organizational citizenship, organizational commitment, productivity, creativity and innovation, self-efficacy, and job satisfaction. Servant-leaders, furthermore, reduce levels of burnout and stress of employees, which ultimately lowers incidences of physical and psychological ill health. Employees working under servant-leaders are also less inclined to leave, which means the organization experiences higher talent retention and attraction, and benefits from a talent advantage in the market.

In summary, self-serving leaders produce a destructive legacy in society, whereas a servant-leader will produce a positive and sustainable legacy, to the benefit of people, organizations, society, and the environment. The differences between the outcomes of a self-serving leader and a servant-leader are summarized in Table 1, below. It is evident from this table that the world needs more servant-leaders and fewer self-serving leaders to resolve the global leadership crisis and to overcome the problems faced by business and society.

Table 1. The self-serving leader versus the servant-leader

Dimension	Self-serving Leader (destructive)	Servant-leader (constructive)
Intent	'Get' mentality (focus on self)	'Give' mentality (focus on others)
Character	Selfishness, jealousy, greed, narcissism, Machiavellianism, personalized charisma, need for power, and psychopathy, which originate from a heart of pride or fear	Courage, altruism, compassion, integrity, accountability, authenticity, humility, and listening, which originate from a heart of love and purpose
Practices	• Abuses positional power to accomplish selfish ambitions • Uses fear, control, and pressure to improve work performance	• Uses positional power to serve others • Uses talent alignment, empowerment, purpose, and support to enhance work performance
Organizational outcomes	• Abuse of organizational resources • Limited organizational performance potential • Exposure of the organization to unethical or unlawful practices (which lead to higher fraud and corruption) • The organization is put at risk • Damage to the reputation of the organization • Poor service delivery • Poor product quality • Decreased productivity • Poor financial results	• Optimized and protected organizational resources (good stewardship) • Enhanced organizational performance through empowerment • Doing business with integrity • Sustainability that reduces organizational risks • Enhanced reputation of the organization • A serving culture that improves customer service • Improved product quality • Enhanced productivity • Improved sales performance • Enhanced financial performance

Individual impact	• Higher employee stress levels • Physical and psychological ill health • Reduced job satisfaction levels of employees • Higher emotional demands • Increased employee turnover • Disengaged employees • Higher employee absenteeism	• Reduced employee burnout and stress • Reduced physical and psychological ill health • Reduced employee turnover intention • Enhanced employee engagement • Enhanced corporate citizenship behavior • Enhanced creativity and innovation • Enhanced organizational commitment • Enhanced self-efficacy • Enhanced job satisfaction • Enhance person–organization fit
Societal outcome	Destructive and limited legacy	A constructive legacy for individuals, the organization, and society

1.7 Defining servant leadership

Servant leadership can be defined as a comprehensive leadership practice that starts with an intent to serve that flows into effective leadership principles and practices to empower people, build high-performing and sustainable organizations, and to create a humane society, while protecting the environment (Coetzer 2018a).

The first element of this definition is that servant leadership is comprehensive. Servant leadership includes components of transformational leadership, transactional leadership, authentic leadership, Level 5 leadership, situational leadership, spiritual leadership, charismatic leadership, and leader–member exchange (Coetzer 2018b). However, servant leadership is also different from these leadership types, as it (a) starts with an intent to serve, (b) serves multiple stakeholders, (c) and includes additional important principles, attributes, and practices that are absent from the other leadership theories. A summary of the similarities between servant leadership and other leadership styles is provided in Table 2, and the differences between servant leadership and other leadership styles are summarized in Table 3.

Table 2. Similarities between servant leadership and other leadership styles (Coetzer 2018b)

Leadership Theory	Similarities with Servant Leadership
Transactional leadership	Focuses on results
	Focuses on people and results
Transformational leadership	Vision, developing followers, and enhancing performance
	Value-based leadership theory
Authentic leadership	Authenticity, role modelling, compassion, integrity, self-awareness, self-regulation, and humility
Level 5 leadership	Focuses first on people, second on strategy
	Humility, accountability, and willingness to learn
Situational leadership	Recognizes follower, leader, and situational relationships
	Provides direction and support
Spiritual leadership	Vision, forgiveness, humility, accountability, courage, integrity, love, and altruism
	Creates meaning, enhances purpose, and cultivates intrinsic motivation
Charismatic leadership	Vision, role modelling, caring, and self-awareness
	Recognizes follower, leader, and situational relationships
Leader–member exchange	Develops trustful relationships with followers

Table 3. Differences between servant leadership and other leadership theories (Coetzer 2018b)

Leadership Theory	Dimension	Servant Leadership
Transactional leadership	Uses practices based on positional power, reward, corrective action, and punishment	Uses practices based on purpose, love, and servanthood
	Uses punishment to correct failure	Uses compassion, understanding, forgiveness, and development to correct failure
	Promotes greed and fear	Promotes the values of unconditional love and purpose
	Unspecified	Develops and empowers followers
	Unspecified	Applies ethical and moral practices
	Focuses mainly on results	Focuses on people and results (but people first)
	Focuses on organizational goals	Focuses on individual, organizational, and societal goals
	Fulfils basic needs of followers	Fulfils basic, psychological, and spiritual needs of followers
Transformational leadership	Focuses mainly on the organization	Focuses mainly on the individual
	Focuses first on results, then people	Focuses first on people, then results
	Enhances performance through motivation	Enhances performance by serving the needs of people
	Main purpose of leader–follower relationship is to attain organizational objectives	Main purpose of leader–follower relationship is talent development and activation
	Individual serves leader	Leader serves individual
	Impacts the individual and organization	Impacts the individual, organization, and society
	Unspecified	Promotes love, altruism, humility, authenticity, forgiveness, and stewardship
Authentic leadership	Unspecified	Serves the individual, organization, and society
	Unspecified	Promotes stewardship and empowerment, developing followers, and creating value for the community

Level 5 leadership	Unspecified	Promotes authenticity, compassion, altruism, stewardship, integrity, listening, empowerment, builds relationships, and has a higher-purpose vision
Situational leadership	Includes components of situational leadership	Includes situational and trait-based leadership components
Spiritual leadership	Unspecified	Promotes authenticity, empowerment, and stewardship, creating value for the community and building internal and external relationships
Charismatic leadership	Unspecified	Promotes ethical and moral characteristics
	Motivates followers emotionally	Motivates followers through service
	Focuses mainly on the organization	Focuses mainly on the individual
	Unspecified	Builds relationships to serve, develop, and empower followers
Leader–member exchange	Unspecified	Displays ethical and moral characteristics
	Focuses on individual relationships	Focuses on individual, team, and community relationships
	Unspecified	Practices personal healing, humility, accountability, and forgiveness in relationships

The second element of the definition of servant leadership is that it starts with an intent to serve. This is the main differentiator between self-serving leaders and servant-leaders. Self-serving leaders can apply any other leadership theory with the wrong intent, which will result in destructive outcomes. However, servant-leaders lead from a desire, motive, and intent to create collective value for multiple stakeholders. The reason why servant-leaders want to lead is because they want to achieve a higher-purpose vision — to create a better world for multiple stakeholders. This service-orientated intent originates from a heart of love and purpose.

The third element servant leadership is effective leadership principles and practices. Servant-leaders evaluate their effectiveness, not in terms of achievement, accumulation, or comfort, but rather by the positive impact they generate for others. Servant-leaders measure success by the long-lasting positive difference they make in people, organizations, society, and the environment. The legacy of servant-leaders generally outlives the lifespan of the leader.

The fourth element of servant leadership is that it serves multiple stakeholders. Servant-leaders serve customers, employees, organizations, shareholders, suppliers, society, and the environment. Servant-leaders always consider all stakeholders in their approach and decision-making, and base their decisions on what is most beneficial for all, including the environment. They continuously serve the needs of multiple stakeholders, and lead people and organizations towards creating a constructive legacy.

The element of multiple stakeholders is absent from all other leadership theories. Self-serving leaders could thus apply any of the other leadership practices to only serve selfish needs or to only serve the needs of shareholders and the organization, to the detriment of employees, suppliers, customers, society, and the environment. Organizations that serve only a single stakeholder's needs to the detriment of other stakeholders are not sustainable, as organizations need multiple stakeholders to survive and to function optimally.

The overall aim of a servant-leader in an organization is to (a) empower employees and ignite individual talent and potential, (b) build a high-performing and sustainable organization that serves people and society through valuable products and services, (c) create a humane society by means of socio-economic development, and to (d) sustain the environment and natural resources for generations to come. The primary roles or functions of a servant-leader are thus to (1) set, translate, and execute a higher-purpose vision, (2) be role models and ambassadors of the higher-purpose vision, (3) align, care for, and grow employees, and (4) continuously monitor and improve (Coetzer, Bussin, & Geldenhuys 2017).

Four analogies can be used to describe the four functions of servant leadership, namely soldier, athlete, farmer, and steward (Coetzer 2018a). A good soldier is someone who diligently strives to achieve a higher-purpose mission, beyond self-interest. An athlete continuously improves to become more effective. A farmer plants and nurtures a seed to ultimately harvest the product of the seed for a greater purpose. A steward manages the belongings of others with accountability, to produce the best return on investment for the owner.

A servant-leader needs to apply the same principles as soldiers, athletes, farmers, and stewards. For example, a servant-leader needs to set a higher-purpose vision and to translate that vision into a mission, strategy, and employee goals. Thereafter, a servant-leader needs to execute the vision by serving employees. A servant-leader needs to continually improve, just like athletes, to become more effective. Servant-leaders also need to find the right talent for the organization, and then create a conducive work environment to activate individual talent and grow and harvest individual talent to achieve the higher-purpose vision of the organization, similarly to farmers, who plant, nurture, and grow seed to harvest a product for a greater good. Servant-leaders need to manage company resources responsibly, in the same way stewards manage the belongings of owners, to produce a decent return.

Each function has specific objectives and principles, as well as required characteristics and competencies. A leadership question is also used in each function to remind the leader what to focus on when deploying the function. A summary of the four functions of servant leadership is provided in Table 4, together with the associated objectives, characteristics, competencies, and leadership question.

Table 4. The functions of a servant-leader (Coetzer 2018a)

	Soldier	Athlete	Farmer	Steward
Leadership question	What is the higher-purpose vision?	How can I improve?	Who needs me?	Who is the owner?
Function	Set, translate, and execute a higher-purpose vision	Become a role model and ambassador	Align, care for, and grow employees	Continuously monitor and improve
Objectives	• Set a higher-purpose vision • Translate a higher-purpose vision into a mission, strategy, and goals • Execute the higher-purpose vision by serving others • Stand up for what is right	• Self-knowledge • Self-management • Self-improvement • Self-revelation • Self-reflection • Staying within the rules	• Align employees • Care for employees • Grow employees	• Apply good stewardship • Monitor performance continuously • Improve products, services, processes, systems, policies, and procedures continuously
Characteristics	• Courage • Altruism	• Authenticity • Humility • Integrity	• Listening • Compassion	• Accountability

Competencies			
• Setting a compelling vision	• Personal capability	• Building relationships • Empowerment	• Stewardship
Strategic servant leadership		Operational servant leadership	
The head of a servant-leader		The hands of a servant-leader	

Domain

The objectives of the soldier-leadership function are: to (a) set a higher-purpose vision, (b) translate the higher-purpose vision into a mission, strategy, and goals, (c) execute the vision by serving others, and (d) stand up for what is right. The characteristics associated with the soldier-leadership function are courage and altruism. The competence requirement for this function is the ability to set a compelling vision. The leadership question used for the soldier-leadership function is: What is the higher-purpose vision?

The objectives of the athlete-leadership function are: (a) self-knowledge, (b) self-management, (c) self-improvement, (d) self-revelation, (e) self-reflection, and (f) staying within the rules. The characteristics associated with this function are authenticity, humility, and integrity. The competency required for the athlete-leadership function is personal capability, which refers to personal effectiveness. The leadership question used for the second function of servant leadership is: How can I improve?

The objectives of the farmer-leadership function are: to (a) align employees, (b) care for and protect employees, and (c) grow employees. This function is supported by the competencies of building relationships and empowerment and the characteristics of listening and compassion. The leadership question that keeps leaders focused in this function is: Who needs me?

The objectives of the steward-leadership function are: to (a) apply good stewardship, (b) monitor performance continuously, and (c) improve products, services, processes, systems, policies, and procedures continuously. The characteristic associated with this function is accountability, and the competency required for this function is stewardship. The leadership question used in the steward-leadership function is: Who is the owner?

The soldier-leadership and athlete-leadership functions can be clustered in a strategic servant-leadership domain (also referred to as the *head* of a servant-leader), and the farmer-leadership and steward-leadership functions can be clustered in the operational servant-leadership domain (also referred to as the *hands* of a servant-leader). Both strategic and operational servant leadership are influenced by the leader's intent, in other words, the reason why a person leads. Servant-leaders lead from a heart of love and purpose, and therefore apply strategic and operational servant leadership from an intent to serve others and with the motive to create a better world for multiple stakeholders. The heart of a servant-leader will thus influence the head and the hands of a servant-leader, in other words, how the leader applies strategic and operational leadership. The intent of a servant-leader (heart) will determine what the leader wants to achieve (head) and how the leader leads others to achieve it (hands). In the following chapters of this book, the *heart*, *head*, and *hands* dimensions of a servant-leader are discussed in more detail, and practical guidelines are provided to apply the four functions effectively in an organization.

1.8 Structure of the book

Chapter 2 discusses the intent of a servant-leader and explains the *heart* dimension of servant leadership in detail. Chapters 3 and 4 focus on the strategic servant leadership functions, namely the soldier-leadership and athlete-leadership functions, and explains the *head* dimension of servant leadership. In Chapters 5 and 6, the farmer-leadership and steward-leadership functions are discussed, which form part of operational servant leadership. These two chapters explain the *hands* dimension of servant leadership. Practical guidelines, resources, and application tools to apply the four functions of servant leadership effectively in any organization or context are provided in these chapters. In Chapter 7, the four servant-leadership functions are consolidated in the Talent Wheel of Servant Leadership, and a framework for cultivating servant-leaders in an organization is provided. The four functions of servant leadership and the Talent Wheel of Servant Leadership are then summarized in a Servant Leadership Model in Chapter 8, and a standard procedure for implementing the Servant Leadership Model in an organization is provided.

PART 1

THE HEART OF A SERVANT-LEADER

(LEADERSHIP INTENT AND VALUES)

CHAPTER 2
THE INTENT AND VALUES OF A SERVANT-LEADER

The *heart* dimension of a leader refers to the intent and values of a leader, which significantly influence a leader's behavior, focus, and approach. It also determines how a leader applies his or her knowledge, skills, and abilities in providing strategic and operational leadership in business or society. The heart of a leader is, furthermore, the main differentiator between a self-serving leader and a servant-leader. Two individuals with the same level of knowledge, skills, ability, potential, and personality could lead vastly differently if they have different leader-heart types or different values. A leader's intent and values will determine how he or she applies knowledge, skills, ability, potential, and personality, which will influence the outcome and results. Hence, different heart styles and values will produce different outcomes and results in business and society. The heart of a leader is the most important aspect of leadership, yet it receives the least attention in leadership theory, practice, and education. It is thus important to understand how different leader-heart types and personal values influence leadership behavior.

2.1 Leader-heart types (leadership intent)

The intent of a leader refers to the reason why a leader wants to lead. The heart of a leader is the foundation from which a person leads. A leader leads from one or more of the following leader-heart types, namely (1) a loving heart, (2) a prideful heart, or a (3) fearful heart.

A loving heart is driven by an intent to serve others and to make a positive difference in the world. Leaders with a loving heart have a 'give' mentality and focus primarily on using their talents, position, knowledge, skills, and attributes to the benefit of others. Such leaders find security and self-worth in serving a higher purpose and contributing to a greater good. They measure success by the positive difference and impact they make in the world. The foundational behaviors associated with a loving heart are: care, trust, proactiveness, and assertiveness.

A prideful heart is driven by an intent to get more for oneself from others, and is generally characterized by a 'get' mentality. A prideful leader primarily focuses on the accumulation of wealth, status, power, and materialistic things, and bases his or her security and self-worth on status. Leaders with a prideful heart measure success in terms of their achievements in life and the approval of others. The foundational behaviors associated with a prideful heart are self-promotion, boasting, egotism, abusiveness, and aggression.

A fearful heart is driven by an intent to guard oneself from others. Leaders with a fearful heart primarily focus on protecting themselves from others, and base their self-worth on experiencing comfort and security. The foundational behaviors associated with a fearful heart are self-protection, hiding, and passiveness. Leaders with a fearful heart measure success in terms of their level of security and comfort.

The measures of success of a prideful or fearful heart (i.e. achievement, approval, and security) cannot always be achieved and cannot fully satisfy a person. For example, there will always be a higher goal or status to achieve in life and more materialistic things to accumulate. It is also not always possible to gain the approval of everybody. Sometimes, people will not approve of you or approve of what you do or stand for. There will, furthermore, be times when a leader needs to stand up for what is right or take a calculated risk. During these times, leaders will most certainly experience discomfort and insecurity. People often associate discomfort and insecurity with failure. However, the truth is that discomfort and insecurity are prerequisites for growth. The only sustainable and truly satisfying measure of success is positive impact — the success measure of a loving heart.

The significance of making a positive impact is that achievement, approval, and security will automatically follow positive impact. For instance, when a loving leader makes time to mentor, coach, and develop direct reports, the overall competence level of the team will increase. Employees are then more capable of sustained high performance, and are less inclined to leave the organization, and the probability of the work unit achieving its goals will increase. This will result in higher team and organizational performance. Achievement, security, and approval will thus increase. Although achievement, security, and approval are not the main intention or goal of the leader, these follow automatically when the leader leads from a loving heart.

A loving heart is the only sustainable approach to leading, as it supports the foundations of business and society. The foundational behaviors associated with a loving heart are care and trust. Businesses are also built on care and trust. For example, investors will only invest money in a business if they trust that the company will produce a decent return. If the organization and its employees truly care about shareholders, they will use these investments wisely to produce a decent return. The foundation of the relationship between shareholder and company is thus care and trust. A company also entrusts employees with its finances, resources, and assets in the hope that they care enough about the company to use it to the benefit of the organization. The foundation of the relationship between employee and employer is thus also care and trust. Furthermore, customers will only buy a company's product or service when they trust that the product or service is of good quality and has value. If a company cares about its customers, it will ensure that a quality and valuable product or service is delivered to the customer. The foundation of the relationship between customer and company is thus, again, care and trust.

The same principles apply in society. For example, parents entrust their children to a school or teacher in the hope that the school or teacher cares enough about them to take good care of their children and to educate their children well. Relationships in society are thus also built on care and trust. From the above, it is clearly evident that a loving heart is the most effective intent with which to lead, as it supports the foundations of business and society.

Sisodia, Sheth, and Wolfe (2014) found that businesses that operated from the principles of love and purpose outperformed other organizations significantly and produced a return of over 1 000% during a ten-year period. Leading from a loving heart is not just the moral way to lead, but also makes good business sense. A summary of the different leader-heart types is provided in Table 5.

Table 5. The three leader-heart types

Dimension	Loving heart	Prideful heart	Fearful heart
Primary focus	Give (others)	Get (self)	Guard (self)
Security and self-worth	Higher purpose	Material things and status	Comfort
Foundational behaviors	Caring Trusting Proactiveness Assertiveness	Self-promotion Boasting Egotism Abuse Aggression	Self-protection Hiding Passiveness
Success measure	Positive impact	Achievement Approval	Security

The heart type of a person will influence his or her leadership behavior, attitude, and focus. As mentioned previously, the heart of the leader is the main differentiator between a self-serving and servant-leader. A self-serving leader will either lead from a prideful or a fearful heart, whereas a servant-leader will lead from a loving heart. The heart of a leader will also influence how a leader applies his or her knowledge, skills, and attributes to provide strategic or operational leadership. For example, a prideful leader will set a vision that only focuses on intrinsic benefits, such as financial performance, shareholder value, a broader market segment, and outperforming competitors. Such a vision serves only select stakeholders. A loving leader, in contrast, will set a higher-purpose vision that focuses on both intrinsic and extrinsic benefits, such as making a positive difference in society, promoting socio-economic development, and creating value for shareholders, employees, suppliers, and customers, all while protecting the environment. Such a vision serves multiple stakeholders. It is therefore important to evaluate a leader's heart, as it is a good predictor of behavior, actions and results.

2.2 Personal values

Personal values flow from a person's heart type. Values are the beliefs and principles that guide one's behavior, judgement, and perception of what is important in life. Personal values determine (a) how a person behaves, (b) what a person perceives as right and wrong, and (c) what a person focuses on in life. For example, if a person values unconditional love, he or she will (a) show empathy and compassion towards others, (b) perceive it as wrong when people are treated inhumanely, and will (c) focus his or her attention on creating value for others. Values influence all aspects of a person's character, such as personality, emotions, and habits.

The analogy of an iceberg can be used to describe how values influence behavior and results. Normally, only the top of an iceberg is visible in the sea. However, the largest part of the iceberg is invisible, below the surface. The same is true about behavior and results. Normally we can only see the behavior of someone and the consequences of that behavior (the results). However, the major aspects that influence behavior, the person's heart, values, personality, thinking patterns, and emotions, are invisible.

Values influence (a) how a person deploys his or her personality, (b) the types of emotions a person experiences, and (c) what a person thinks about. Behavior (personality), emotions, and thinking patterns then produce a certain result or outcome. For instance, negative behaviors (such as aggression), emotions (such as fear), and thinking patterns (such as self-doubt) will produce a negative outcome when someone needs to resolve conflict, whereas positive behaviors (such as compassion), emotions (such as fulfillment), and thinking patterns (such as optimism) will produce a positive outcome in the same scenario. It is therefore important to understand the different types of values, as these influence behavior, emotions, and thinking patterns, which ultimately cause a specific result or outcome.

According to Barret (2006), values can be categorized into seven clusters (also known as 'the seven levels of consciousness'), namely survival, relationships, self-esteem, transformation, internal cohesion, making a difference, and service. These value clusters are presented in Table 6. This table also depicts the heart type from which the values in each cluster originate.

Table 6. The seven value clusters or levels of consciousness (Barret 2006)

Origin	Level	Value cluster	Focus
Loving heart	7	Service	Leading a life of selfless service
	6	Making a difference	Making a positive difference in the world
	5	Internal cohesion	Finding meaning in existence
'Heart transplant'	4	Transformation	Finding freedom by letting go of fears about survival, feeling loved, and being respected
Prideful or fearful heart	3	Self-esteem	Feeling a sense of personal self-worth
	2	Relationships	Feeling safe, respected, and loved
	1	Survival	Satisfying physical needs

The low-level value clusters — survival, relationships, and self-esteem — are related to a prideful or fearful heart, and focuses on promoting self-interests, whereas the high-level value clusters — internal cohesion, making a difference, and service — are related to a loving heart, and focuses on the interests of others and the common good. *Survival* is the first low-level value cluster, where the focus is on satisfying one's physical needs. *Relationships* is the second low-level value cluster, and here the focus is on feeling safe, respected, and loved. *Self-esteem* is the third low-level value cluster, where the focus is on having a sense of self-worth.

People generally start off in life by focusing on values in the low-level value clusters. Later, as they mature, they adopt values in the upper-level value clusters. Some form of *transformation* (Value cluster 4) is usually needed to initiate this change in a person's life perspective. During the transformation phase, people experience a 'heart transplant' and let go of pride and fear about survival, as well as the need to feel loved and respected, and adopt values from the upper-level value clusters.

The fifth value cluster is *Internal cohesion*, where the focus is on finding a higher life purpose and meaning in one's existence. The sixth value cluster is *Making a difference,* where the aim is to build a positive legacy. The seventh value cluster is *Service*, which is selfless service of others. The values in the high-level value clusters normally originate from a loving heart.

It is important to mention that a person should have a balanced consciousness across all seven value clusters. People who only focus on the high-level value clusters may lose sight of their physical and emotional needs, whereas people who only focus on the low-level value clusters may lose sight of the bigger picture of living a life of service and significance. A servant-leader, thus, leads from a loving heart in making a difference in the world by living a life of significance and serving others selflessly, while at the same time meeting his or her physical and emotional needs.

A leader should be aware of the values that drive his or her leadership behaviors, emotions, and thinking patterns, and be sure to adopt values across all seven value clusters. One way to discover one's personal values is to complete a values assessment. The Personal Values Assessment of the Barrett Values Centre may be useful in this regard.

2.3 Organizational values

Organizational values are the beliefs and principles that guide employee behavior, judgement, and focus. Organizational values can be grouped into the same value clusters as personal values. These organizational value clusters are presented in Table 7.

Table 7. Organizational value clusters or levels
of consciousness (Barret 2006)

Origin	Level	Value cluster	Focus
Loving leader	7	Service	Caring for humanity, future generations, and the planet
	6	Making a difference	Cooperating with and forming alliances with others
	5	Internal cohesion	Aligning employees to a shared vision, mission, and values
Leader-heart transplant	4	Transformation	Involving employees and giving them a voice in decision-making

	3	Self-esteem	Creating order, performance, and effectiveness that will generate respect and group pride
Prideful or Fearful leaders	2	Relationships	Building harmonious internal relationships that will create a sense of belonging
	1	Survival	Establishing conditions of financial stability and safety for group members

Organizations with values in the lower-level clusters focus on creating financial stability (survival), good internal relationships and a sense of belonging for employees (relationships), and high performance and effectiveness (self-esteem). Organizational values in the low-level value clusters usually originate from fearful or prideful leaders. Organizations that focus only on the lower-level value clusters can be called self-serving organizations. These organizations have an inward focus and only concentrate on self-interests. Self-serving organizations focus primarily on (a) being better than the competitor, (c) becoming the largest and greatest in the market, (d) attaining the leading market share, and (e) producing the biggest financial returns for shareholders, without adding any significant value to the benefit of people, other organizations, society, or the environment.

Organizations with values in the upper-level value clusters focus on (a) aligning employees to a higher-purpose vision, mission, and values (internal cohesion), (b) cooperating with and forming alliances with other organizations (making a difference), and (c) serving humanity, future generations, and the planet (service). These organizational values originate from loving leaders in the organization. Organizations that only focus on the high-level value clusters are usually non-profit organizations. These organizations have an outward focus, and primarily aim to create value for employees, customers, other organizations, and society, but sometimes neglect to consider their survival.

A servant-organization has values across all seven value clusters. These organizations have an outward-in focus and aim to create significant value for multiple stakeholders (customers, employees, shareholders, suppliers, and society) by generating good profits while maintaining the environment. These organizations focus on people, profit, and the planet. Servant-organizations significantly outperform self-serving organizations, because they function as part of an ecosystem. The organization serves society, and society, in return, supports the organization. The organization serves its employees, and the employees serve the organization. The organization serves its shareholders, and the shareholders invest in the organization. The organization serves its customers, and the customers buy from the organization. The organization protects the environment, and the environment provides the natural resources for the organization to survive. Leaders are responsible for building servant-organizations by embedding balanced values in organizations, from a loving heart.

PART 2

THE HEAD OF A SERVANT-LEADER

(STRATEGIC SERVANT LEADERSHIP)

The *heart* dimension of a servant-leader was discussed in Part 1 of this book. The next section focuses on the *head* dimension of servant leadership, and explains the two related functions, namely soldier-leadership and athlete-leadership. These two functions are discussed in separate chapters (Chapters 3 and 4). Practical guidelines are provided to apply the soldier- and athlete-leadership functions effectively in any organization.

CHAPTER 3
THE SOLDIER-LEADERSHIP FUNCTION

The first function of a servant-leader is to set, translate, and execute a higher-purpose vision. This function falls within the strategic servant-leadership domain, also known as the *head* dimension of servant leadership. The analogy of a soldier is used to describe this function.

A soldier is one of the most selfless occupations or positions a person could fulfil. A soldier will leave his or her family, spouse, children, personal comfort, and safety to participate in a higher-purpose mission, to the benefit of others. A soldier first establishes a greater-good mission and then consistently focuses on achieving that mission. Such a mission always focuses on the benefit of others, either by protecting others, fighting for the rights of others, saving the lives of others, or striving to provide a better quality of life for others. Once a higher-purpose mission has been set, a soldier does everything in his or her power to accomplish it. Soldiers will use their talents, position, and power to serve the higher-purpose mission, and often do it at great personal cost. A soldier will also willingly help, support, and serve other soldiers to achieve the higher-purpose mission. Ideal soldiers are, furthermore, brilliant at execution, and will constantly measure their progress and success. Soldiers are courageous and selfless. They are not afraid to face danger or to enter risky and uncomfortable scenarios to achieve a mission greater than themselves.

The heart or intent of a soldier influences a soldier's behavior and practice. For example, a soldier driven by a loving heart will always strive for peace and reconciliation first, but will engage in combat if peace and reconciliation are not possible, to (a) protect the interest of others,

(b) maintain morality, or (c) conquer evil. However, soldiers driven by a prideful or fearful heart will engage in combat to accomplish selfish motives, such as territorial gain. These soldiers are not considered good or moral. The heart of a soldier will thus influence his or her behavior and intent. A good and moral soldier will always evaluate his or her heart's intent or motive before acting.

The same principles apply to leadership. Leaders need to set a compelling vision that focuses primarily on the interests of others, the greater good. This vision should be set from a loving heart, and not from a prideful or fearful heart. Once a higher-purpose vision has been set, a leader needs to translate this vision into a mission, strategy, and employee goals. A leader should also focus on execution by serving and supporting employees to achieve the higher-purpose vision. It does not make sense to set and translate a higher-purpose vision without executing it. The execution phase is most important. Leaders must therefore use their talents, position, and positional power to serve, empower, and help employees to achieve the higher-purpose vision. Leaders should, furthermore, stand up for what is right.

Some of the characteristics that leaders should possess to be effective in this function are altruism and courage. Leaders should be selfless and have a desire make a positive difference in the world, to the benefit of others. Leaders should also be courageous to stand up for what is right in business, government, and society. Both altruism and courage are thus required to set a higher-purpose vision and to translate and execute it effectively.

A question that could be used to remind a leader of the soldier-leadership function is: What is the higher-purpose vision? This question will enable the leader to keep the vision in sight and focus on its execution. A summary of the objectives, characteristics, competencies, and leadership question of the soldier-leadership function is provided in Table 8, below. This chapter discusses each objective in more detail, and provides practical guidelines and application tools to apply these principles in the workplace.

Table 8. The objectives, characteristics, and competency of the soldier-leadership function (Coetzer et al. 2017)

Function	Set, translate, and execute a higher-purpose vision
Leadership question	What is the higher-purpose vision?
Objectives	• Set a higher-purpose vision • Translate the vision into a mission, strategy, and goals • Execute the vision by serving others • Stand up for what is right
Characteristics	• Courage • Altruism
Competency	• Compelling vision

3.1 Set a higher-purpose vision

The first objective of the soldier-leadership function is to set a higher-purpose vision from a loving heart. Before a higher purpose can be set, a leader must understand what the higher purpose of business is and why it is important.

Business is like an ecosystem. Any business originates from identifying a customer need and developing a product or service to satisfy that need. A business cannot exist without a customer. A business also uses some form of environmental or natural resource to produce a product or service. All life depends on environmental and natural resources for survival. An organization is also dependent on environmental and natural resources to survive and to be sustainable over time. A business furthermore needs people (employees) to (a) develop a product or service, (b) serve customers, and to (c) manage the business. The customer will not experience the organization itself when buying a product or service, but will rather experience the employee (the person) serving them, or experience the product the employee produced. Employees are thus the closest to both the product and the customer. A business additionally needs suppliers to co-create a product or service. The products and services of other companies are therefore required to produce the organization's final product or service. Finally, a business needs shareholders to invest capital in the company. It would be difficult for a company to grow without this investment. Business is therefore dependent on people (customers, employees, and shareholders), other companies (suppliers), and the environment for survival.

Although an organization needs customers, employees, suppliers, shareholders, and the environment to survive, the converse is also true. Customers, employees, suppliers, shareholders, and the environment also need businesses to survive. For example, a customer will not have the money to buy a product or service if he or she is not employed. People need employment in order to earn an income, to be able to buy the products and services of companies, and companies need customers (people) with money to buy their products and services. Organizations therefore have a moral and economic responsibility to create employment opportunities for people. The same principle applies to suppliers. To survive, suppliers need other companies to buy their products and services, and organizations need suppliers to co-create and deliver a final product or service to the customer. Organizations therefore have a moral and economic responsibility to create partnership opportunities for other companies (suppliers). Shareholders are also dependent on the businesses they invest in to make a good return, and businesses are dependent on shareholders for working capital. Shareholders cannot receive a return on their investment without businesses, and businesses cannot grow without shareholders. Businesses therefore have a moral and economic responsibility to produce a good return for shareholders. Businesses furthermore need environmental resources to produce a product or service. If natural resources are not preserved and protected in the present, business will not survive in the future. Organizations thus have a moral and economic responsibility to protect the environment and to preserve natural resources, to ensure businesses can continue in the future. It is therefore clear all stakeholders are interdependent on each other for survival. A graphical display of this interdependence is shown in Figure 1.

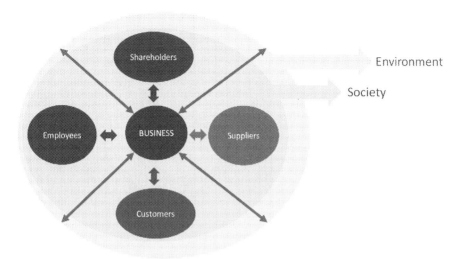

Figure 1. Business Interdependence Model

Customers, employees, suppliers, and shareholders are all human beings — people living in society. Businesses need people and society for survival, and people and society need businesses for survival. The true purpose of business is thus to serve people and society while protecting the environment. However, it seems that businesses have lost perspective over the years. Organizations often focus on generating more profit, at the expense of people, society, and the environment. For example, many organizations retrench people or replace them with machines to make more profit, without consideration of the larger impact on people, society, or the future sustainability of the business. A report from the World Economic Forum (2016) indicated that approximately 5.1 million jobs will be lost between 2015 and 2020 to artificial intelligence, robotics, nanotechnology, 3-D printing, and biotechnology. Another report indicated that 47% of employed people in the United States of America are at risk of becoming unemployed due to computerization (Frey & Osborne 2017). These statistics raise several questions about the ecosystem of business, for instance: What is the main focus or intent of current organizations? Is the main focus on serving people and society, or is it on generating more profit at the expense of people and society? Is this business approach sustainable when taking into consideration that businesses are dependent on people and society for survival?

To sustain business, society, and the environment, now and in the future, organizations should focus on serving and creating value for multiple stakeholders (customers, employees, suppliers, shareholders, society, and the environment) while making a decent profit. Profit should be perceived as the means to create value, and not as the value itself. Profit is like oxygen. A person needs oxygen to survive, but the purpose of living is much greater than getting oxygen. The same principle applies for profit. A business needs profit to survive; however, the purpose of business is much greater than making a profit. An organization should thus not focus only on high performance, but also on high significance. Both performance and significance are required to sustain a business into the future. The way to refocus a business on its true purpose is to set a higher-purpose vision, one that goes beyond profit.

A higher-purpose vision is the ideal state, in which the organization's core purpose and capability are aligned to the needs of people and society, with the aim of creating and sustaining a better world for current and future generations. The higher-purpose vision statement of a company describes how the organization will create value for multiple stakeholders (customers, employees, shareholders, suppliers, society, and the environment), now and in the future. A higher-purpose vision statement should therefore include a description of the (a) purpose of the organization, (b) alignment of the company's products and services to the needs of people and society, and the (c) type of legacy the organization wants to create in the future.

The following questions might be useful in drafting a higher-purpose vision for an organization:

- What is the true purpose of the organization?
- Why does the organization exist?
- How will the organization create value for multiple stakeholders (now and in the future)?
- How will the organization improve and sustain the world to the benefit of all?
- What type of needs exist in society? How will the organization fulfil these needs?
- What legacy does the organization plan to leave?

3.2 Translate the vision into a mission, a strategy, and goals

Once the higher-purpose vision has been set, the leader must translate the vision into a mission, a strategy, and goals. This is the second objective of the soldier-leadership function. The translation process consists of four phases (Coetzer et al. 2017):

1. Translate the higher-purpose vision into a mission, a strategy, and goals.
2. Establish the business processes, systems, and policies to enable the vision, mission, strategy, and goals.
3. Establish the capability and capacity frameworks to support the vision, mission, strategy, and goals.
4. Align employees with the business processes, systems, and policies, as well as to the capability and capacity frameworks.

The four phases of this translation process are summarized in Figure 2, below.

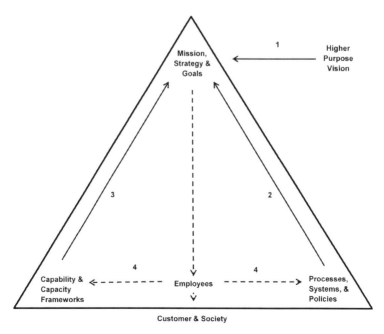

Figure 2. Translation process and phases (Coetzer et al. 2017)

In **Phase 1**, the leader should translate the higher-purpose vision into a (a) mission statement, (b) company and work-unit strategy, and (c) employee goals, in that order. The mission, strategy, and goals of the company should focus, firstly, on the customer and society — because that is why the organization exists — and, secondly, on employees, because employees produce the product and serve the customer.

A mission statement describes the focus of the organization, in other words, on what the organization will consistently focus to achieve the higher-purpose vision. A strategy describes the aim of the organization or the work unit. An organizational strategy is the summary of the strategic objectives the organization aims to achieve in the next two to five years in support of the higher-purpose vision. The strategy also includes the measures of success and specific timelines. A work-unit strategy also consists of these elements, and must, furthermore, be in line with the organizational strategy and the higher-purpose vision of the company. Goals are then set for each employee, in line with the departmental or work-unit strategy.

In short, the higher-purpose vision should be translated into a company mission and strategy. The company strategy should then be translated into departmental or work unit strategies, and the departmental or work-unit strategies should thereafter be translated into specific employee goals. In this way, the employee knows exactly how his or her work contributes towards achieving the higher-purpose vision of the organization, which makes work meaningful.

In **Phase 2**, the leader should develop the business processes, systems, and policies to enable the organization to achieve the vision, mission, strategy, and goals. A business process is a series of activities to deliver a product or service, or to create value, in line with the higher-purpose vision, mission, and strategy of the company. Systems are the computers or other systems used to organize, monitor, and store information. Systems are used to optimize or automate the activities of a business process and to measure progress. Policies are the governing principles and rules that guide decision-making and behavior in the organization. Once the vision, mission, strategy, and goals have been set, the leader must establish the governing principles and rules to guide employee behavior and decision-making in the organization, in support of the higher-purpose vision, mission, and strategy. This will ensure that the set boundaries for behavior in the organization are aligned with achieving the higher-purpose vision.

In **Phase 3**, the leader should develop Capability and Capacity Frameworks to support the higher-purpose vision, mission, strategy, and goals of the company. A Capability Framework reflects the knowledge, skills, and attributes required to attain the higher-purpose vision, mission, and strategy. This is also called a *competency framework*.

A Capacity Framework lists the number and type of positions required in the organization to execute the higher-purpose vision, mission, and strategy. Once the number and types of positions have been established, the positions can be profiled to indicate the purpose, responsibilities, and requirements of each position. The purpose and responsibilities of a position derive from the relevant business processes, and the requirements of a position derive from the Capability Framework (i.e. the knowledge, skills, and attributes required to be successful in a position). The Job Profiles can then be used in recruitment, selection, talent management, learning and development, and performance management processes to align individual purpose and talent to the purpose and requirements of a position.

In **Phase 4**, employees should be aligned to the business processes, systems, and policies, as well as to the Capacity and Capability Frameworks of the organization. For example, when a new business process, system, or policy is introduced in the organization, the leader should initiate and facilitate a proper change management process to (a) make employees aware of the change, (b) create understanding why the change is necessary and important, and to (c) ensure employees successfully adopt and implement the change. In this way, employees embrace the new system, process, or policy.

A leader should also align employees to the Capacity and Capability Frameworks of the organization. The leader can use the Job Profiles (that originated from the Capacity and Capability Frameworks) in recruitment, selection, learning and development, talent management, and performance management processes. For example, the leader could use a Job Profile in a learning and development process by comparing an employee's current knowledge, skills, attributes, and life purpose with the required knowledge, skills, attributes, and purpose of a position, to determine any learning and development gaps. A Personal Development Plan can then be implemented for the employee, to close the gaps in his or her knowledge, skills, or attributes. A re-evaluation can be done afterwards, to determine whether the learning and development activities were successful in closing the identified gaps. The leader could also use the Job Profiles in recruitment and selection processes to identify the best person–job fit for vacant positions, and in talent management processes to identify person–job fit for future positions. In this way, employees are aligned to the Capacity and Capability Frameworks of the organization, which supports the higher-purpose vision of the company.

A strategic alignment template (Tool 1: Strategic Alignment Matrix) is provided in Appendix A. This application tool can be used to translate the higher-purpose vision of the organization into a company mission and strategy, as well as departmental or work-unit strategies and employee goals. It also summarizes the translation of information, indicating how each employee goal links to the higher-purpose vision of the organization.

3.3 Execute the vision by serving others

The third objective of the soldier-leadership function is to execute the vision by serving others. Once the higher-purpose vision has been set and translated, the leader needs to focus on execution by enabling employees to achieve the higher-purpose vision. Leaders should help, support, empower, motivate, and fulfil the needs of employees to achieve the higher-purpose vision. In other words, leaders should serve and empower employees to achieve the higher-purpose vision, mission, and strategy of the organization. Employees should not serve leaders, but rather the higher-purpose vision. When employees serve leaders, the higher-purpose vision might suffer. However, when leaders serve employees, the leader and the employees work as partners in achieving the higher-purpose vision of the company, and the probability of success becomes greater.

3.4 Stand up for what is right

The fourth objective of the soldier-leadership function is to stand up for what is right. Leaders must protect the interest of others. They must ensure that justice prevails in the organization, and that ethical and moral standards are upheld. Leaders should thus continuously monitor whether the best interests of multiple others are protected.

When leaders become aware of any unfairness, immorality, or unethical practices in business governance or society, they must (a) investigate the matter thoroughly to determine what the causes are, (b) apply their mind to initiate the best possible solution, to the benefit of multiple stakeholders, (c) implement effective interventions to resolve the issue, and (d) evaluate the success of the intervention.

A loving heart will motivate a leader to stand up for what is right. If a leader genuinely cares about his or her employees, he or she will protect their interests. However, when a leader is driven by pride or fear, he or she will use employees to achieve selfish goals or to protect self-interests. A fearful or prideful heart will thus prevent a leader from standing up for what is right.

A leader with a loving heart will look after the interests of others and will do everything in his or her power to ensure that fairness and morality prevail. However, prideful or fearful leaders will either be too selfish or too afraid to put themselves in jeopardy by standing up for others. A loving heart is thus the core motive to stand up for what is right.

3.5 Characteristics and competencies of the soldier-leadership function

Two characteristics support the four objectives of the soldier-leadership function, namely altruism and courage. Altruism can be defined as being others-orientated and selfless, with a desire to positively influence and help others to become more successful in life by consistently serving their needs. Altruistic individuals strive to make a positive difference in people, organizations, and society, and to leave a constructive legacy in the world, beyond their own lifetime. A leader needs to be altruistic in setting a higher-purpose vision for an organization. It would be impossible to set a higher-purpose vision if the leader is not 'others-orientated' and does not desire to make a positive difference in the world.

Once a higher-purpose vision has been set, the leader needs courage to translate and execute it. Courage is also needed to stand up for what is right. Courage can be defined as the fearlessness to defend what is morally right, despite adversity, and to take calculated risks. Courage is not necessarily the absence of fear, but the channeling thereof to achieve a greater good. Leaders will find it difficult to execute a higher-purpose vision and to stand up for what is right if they do not possess courage. Altruism and courage originate from a loving leader-heart.

The competency associated with the soldier-leadership function is being able to create a compelling vision. This can be defined as the ability to (a) conceptualize a higher-purpose vision, (b) link past events and current trends with potential future scenarios, and to (c) create value for organizations, their employees, and for society, now and in the future.

CHAPTER 4
THE ATHLETE-LEADERSHIP FUNCTION

The second function of a servant-leader is to become a role model and ambassador. This function is also part of strategic servant leadership, which is the *head* dimension of servant leadership. The analogy of an athlete is used to describe this function.

Professional athletes know their individual talents, and they continuously strive to improve their performance by means of (a) continuous training and development, (b) applying exceptional self-discipline to manage their emotional, mental, and physical state, and by (c) activating their talents within a set of rules or regulations. They also evaluate their performance regularly, and find ways to enhance their performance and effectiveness.

A first principle in being an athlete is self-knowledge. A professional athlete continuously evaluates his or her own strengths and development areas, to either capitalize on strengths or to overcome development areas. Professional athletes also know their talents. For example, a professional boxer will know that he or she is not necessarily equipped to be a 100m-sprint athlete and will fail in competing on the track. However, when a professional boxer enters a boxing ring, he or she will flourish, because that is his or her talent and strength.

The same principle applies to leadership. A leader should know his or her personal strengths and development areas, in order to align these strengths to a specific role or position to achieve a higher-purpose vision. A leader should also, just like athletes, continuously reflect on his or her own leadership behavior, to determine how he or she can further improve and become even more effective as a leader. A leader will fail if he or she tries to fit into a role that is not aligned to his or her true purpose and talents, the same way a boxer will fail when trying to compete against 100m-sprint athletes. However, a leader will flourish when he or she aligns personal purpose and talents to a specific leadership role.

A second principle in being a professional athlete is to manage one's physical, mental, and emotional state. Athletes train for hours every day to improve their physical state and performance. They will wake up early in the morning to exercise, while others are still sleeping, and will apply extraordinary self-discipline to keep to their exercise routines. Athletes also adhere to stringent eating plans to ensure optimal physical strength. Athletes furthermore manage their conscious thoughts, to ensure they maintain a highly positive mental state. Physical performance often starts with constructive thoughts and a positive mental state. Athletes regularly visualize how they successfully execute a task. They train and prepare their minds for success prior to an event. A positive mental state then enables them to perform consistently. Professional athletes also manage their emotional state. They train themselves not to be influenced by their emotions and not to react to external stimuli in pressurized situations, such as negative comments by supporters when they've made a mistake during an important sporting event.

The same principle applies to leadership. Leaders need to manage their physical, mental, and emotional state in order to perform optimally. They also need to manage their physical state, to ensure they have the energy to lead and serve others. They should focus their mind on constructive thought patterns, in order to behave in a manner that serves a higher-purpose vision. Leaders also need to be in the right mental state to become role models for others in achieving a higher-purpose vision. Leaders, furthermore, need to manage their emotional state, to behave consistently in pressurized situations. Managing one's physical, mental, and emotional state takes time, effort, and self-discipline. It is therefore important for a leader to be able to manage his or her own physical, mental, and emotional state before he or she leads and serve others. Effective leadership starts with good self-leadership.

The third principle an athlete adheres to is to continuously improve. Once athletes have identified their strengths and development areas, they focus their attention and effort on self-improvement. This is done by, firstly, establishing a training and development plan and, secondly, applying the self-discipline to put the development plan in action. Athletes also measure their improvement continuously, to determine whether the training and development plan was successful.

The same principle is applicable to leadership. Once leaders have identified their personal strengths and development areas, they need to establish a Personal Development Plan to activate their strengths and overcome their development areas. Thereafter, they need to apply the self-discipline to put the Personal Development Plan into action and then continuously measure their improvement.

A fourth principle of being an athlete is to reveal true personal talent. Athletes know they will fail if they try to adopt someone else's strength instead of harnessing their own potential. Good athletes activate their natural potential and strengths, while recognizing their weaknesses, because they understand that their individual talents and strengths are different from others' and constitute a competitive advantage. Professional athletes are thus authentic in applying their talents to succeed.

Leaders should also reveal their true potential, talents, strengths, and weaknesses. This will enable them to align their talents and potential to specific leadership roles and to align the talents and strengths of others to their own weaknesses. Often, leaders believe that a sign of weakness reflects poor leadership, which is far from the truth. A true leader reveals his or her personal weaknesses honestly and openly, and will bridge personal weaknesses with the strengths and talents of others. In this way, the probability of success increases, which is a result of good leadership. Leaders should thus be authentic in their leadership approach and reveal their true potential and development areas.

A fifth principle in being an athlete is self-reflection. An athlete will always reflect on personal performance after a sporting event, to determine what was done well and what could be done to excel. An athlete will discover personal development areas through self-reflection sessions and initiate personal development actions to improve performance. An athlete will then self-reflect after the next sporting event, to determine whether the actions he or she applied improved personal performance.

Leaders should also practice self-reflection regularly, reflecting on their leadership behavior and effectiveness. Leaders should regularly reflect on what they did well and how they can excel in their leadership approach, behavior, and effectiveness. Repeated self-reflection will assist leaders to identify personal development areas and address these to become more effective leaders. Once personal development areas have been identified, a leader can put the necessary development actions in practice to improve his or her leadership behavior. The success of the personal development actions can then be determined in a next self-reflection session.

A final principle in being an athlete is to stay within the rules. Athletes know they will be disqualified or given a red card when they contravene the rules of the game. Good athletes therefore activate and execute their talents within the boundaries of the rules. The same principle applies to leadership. Leaders need to activate their talents in line with ethical behavior and moral business practices. Leaders also know that, when they behave unethically, they will face disciplinary action or even be removed from their position.

Have you ever wondered why an athlete competes in a sporting event knowing that he or she will not win? For example, many athletes who competed against Usain Bolt in the Olympic Games knew their chances of winning were slim. Why then compete? Professional athletes know they will not always win, but they strive to continuously improve. A leader's perspective should be similar. A leader should not focus on winning or being better than others. This type of behavior normally originates from a prideful heart. No, leaders should aim to improve themselves continuously to better serve people, organizations, and societies and to make themselves more capable of leaving a long-lasting, positive legacy in the world, for the benefit of others. Hence, the question leaders should continuously ask themselves is: How can I improve?

The objectives, characteristics, and competencies of the athlete-leadership function are summarized in Table 9 and are discussed in more detail below.

Table 9. The objectives, characteristics, and competencies of the athlete-leadership function (Coetzer et al. 2017)

Function	Become a role model and ambassador
Leadership question	How can I improve?

Objectives	• Self-knowledge
	• Self-management
	• Self-improvement
	• Self-revelation
	• Self-reflection
	• Stay within the rules
Characteristics	• Authenticity
	• Humility
	• Integrity
Competency	• Personal capability

4.1 Self-knowledge

The first objective of the athlete-leadership function is self-knowledge. Self-knowledge refers to knowing one's heart (values, personality, and work passion), head (cognitive ability), and hands (knowledge, skills, and natural talents). In Chapter 2, values were defined as the beliefs and principles that guide behavior, judgement, and one's perception of what is important in life. In other words, personal values determine how a person behaves, what a person perceives as right and wrong, and what a person focuses on in life. The different types of values were also discussed in Chapter 2, namely survival, relationships, self-esteem, transformation, internal cohesion, making a difference, and selfless service.

4.1.1 Knowing one's heart

Values, personality, and work passion are all considerations in knowing one's heart. When leaders know their heart, they understand why they lead and why they behave in a certain manner. Leaders should thus, firstly, know their values, as these influence their personal behavior, judgement, and life perception. Personal values also determine how someone leads others. Leaders must know the type of values they hold dear, in order to understand their level of consciousness across the value clusters.

One way to become aware of personal values is to complete a Personal Values Assessment and to reflect on the results. The Personal Values Assessment of the Barrett Values Centre (www.valuescentre.com) may be useful in this regard. This assessment evaluates personal values across all the clusters, and reveals any consciousness blind spots. The results of this assessment can be used to identify value strengths and development areas, which could then be used to formulate a Personal Development Plan to adopt the productive values that are necessary for effective leadership.

Leaders should, secondly, understand why they behave in a certain manner. Personality, knowledge, skills, and the environment all influence how a person behaves. For example, personal values influence an individual's personality, and a person's personality will determine how he or she (1) interacts with other people, (2) applies his or her mind at work, and (3) copes in difficult circumstances, which will inevitably influence his or her leadership behavior and effectiveness. Behavior is also influenced by a person's knowledge, skills, and abilities. For instance, when someone receives training on how to build better relationships with others or to deal with conflict more effectively, that person becomes able to amend his or her behavior accordingly, which will improve his or her leadership behavior and effectiveness. Another factor that influences behavior is the environment or situation. For example, under normal circumstances, an empathetic person will not hurt another person physically. However, if a criminal threatens that person's family, that person will behave differently and even harm the criminal physically to protect his or her family.

A leader should, thirdly, know his or her work passion, which includes personal interests and life purpose. Interests are the tasks or activities a person enjoys doing, and a life purpose is the reason why an individual exists. Work passion generally originates from a person's life purpose, and includes personal interests — those activities a person will do voluntarily, without any form of recognition or reward. Leaders have to know their life purpose and work passion in order to align these effectively to a job or leadership role. People experience feelings of emptiness, life dissatisfaction, and meaninglessness when their daily work is not aligned to their life purpose and work passion. People then try to compensate for this misalignment in unproductive ways, such as accumulating money to buy more material things, achieving higher goals to gain recognition, in order to feel valued, or using alcohol or drugs to experience some form of short-term pleasure. They may also embark on adventures to get away from daily life, become dependent on others for their happiness, or try to find life satisfaction in any other materialistic or external source. These efforts to compensate for misalignment rarely succeed, and often lead to more dissatisfaction and feelings of insignificance. Leaders should therefore discover their life purpose and know their work passion, so that they can align it to a daily work and experience high levels of life satisfaction and life significance.

An Individual Passion and Purpose Guide is provided in Appendix A. This guide can be used to conceptualize a work passion statement and to draft a life purpose declaration. Once leaders have compiled a work passion statement and life purpose declaration, they can use these statements as a benchmark to align work accordingly.

4.1.2   Knowing one's head

The second dimension leaders should become aware of is understanding one's cognitive ability. This is part of the *head* dimension of leadership. Cognitive ability refers to a person's ability, inclination, and preference to (1) work in a specific context or work domain, (2) solve problems, and (3) learn new information. According to Prinsloo and Prinsloo (2012), there are five general types of work domains, namely pure operational, diagnostic accumulation, tactical strategy, parallel processing, and pure strategic. These work domains are listed on a continuum of (a) structure versus chaos, (b) short-term versus long-term orientation, (c) practical versus theoretical, and (e) operational versus strategic. People with a strong ability to work in a *pure operational* context (a) prefer structure, (b) focus on achieving results in the short term (1–3 months), (c) are practical in their approach, and (d) flourish in operational jobs. People with *pure strategic* abilities (a) can work in chaos (unstructured environment), (b) focus on the long term (5+ years), (c) are theoretical in their approach, and (d) flourish in strategic jobs. People in the middle of the continuum, the *tactical strategy* domain, are able to translate a strategy and coordinate activities to make a strategy practical. People located within this domain also possess strengths to improve processes, systems, and procedures. The *diagnostic accumulation* domain refers to the ability and inclination to identify ways to improve execution by means of continuous analysis, diagnosis, and expert intervention. These people can identify underlying patterns and create future models or scenarios of work. The *diagnostic accumulation* domain falls in the middle of the *operational* range of the *work domain* continuum. The *parallel processing* domain, on the other hand, falls in the middle of the *strategic* range of the *work domain* continuum. It is important to note that cognitive ability is not the same as intellectual intelligence (IQ). For example, medical doctors, who are highly intelligent people, fall within the *pure operational* work domain, because they need to be precise and accurate in their work and must function within rigid parameters.

In an organization, only a few individuals are needed in the *pure strategic* domain; they are needed to evaluate past, current, and future trends to guide the company to future sustainability. More employees are required in the *pure operational* domain, as this is where value is physically created and the strategy and vision of the company become a reality.

Figure 3, below, provides a graphical display of the strengths of each work domain. With reference to servant leadership, people situated within the *pure strategic* domain are good at setting a higher-purpose vision for an organization. People within the *parallel processing* and *tactical strategy* domains are effective at translating the higher-purpose vision into functional or departmental strategies and employee goals. People within the *diagnostic accumulation* and *pure operational* domains are excellent at execution, in other words, making the higher-purpose vision a reality.

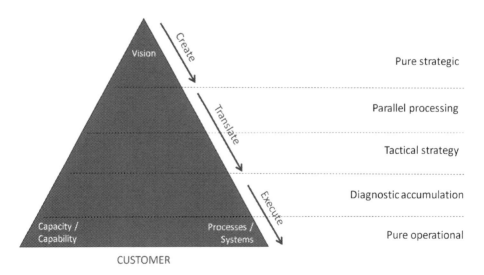

Figure 3. Cognitive strengths

One way to become aware of one's cognitive strengths is to complete a cognitive ability assessment such as the Cognitive Processing Profile (CPP) developed by Prinsloo and Prinsloo (2012). The CPP assessment identifies a person's strengths in terms of the five work domains, and provides insightful information on how a person solves problems and learns new information. A leader can then use the results of the CPP report to align his or her cognitive strengths with a position or role within an organization or society. In this way, a leader could capitalize on his or her strengths and become more effective as a leader.

4.1.3   *Knowing one's hands*

Leaders should, thirdly, know their hands, in other words, their specific knowledge, skills, and natural talent. Knowledge is obtained from completing educational programs or short courses, and refers to the expertise a person possesses. Skills are the abilities a person possesses, and are generally gained through experiential learning or practical experience. Natural talents are those things a person can do with ease, with which others may struggle. It is important for a leader to know his or her specific knowledge, skills, and natural talents to effectively align these to the requirements of a job or position within an organization. In this way, leaders can capitalize on their strengths to become more effective.

A person's education and experience record are normally a good indicator of the knowledge, skills, and natural talent a person possesses. The Individual Passion and Purpose Guide in Appendix A might also be useful to discover personal strengths in terms of knowledge, skills, and natural talents. Leaders can use the questions in this guide to reflect on the expert knowledge, skills, and natural talents they possess.

4.2 Self-management

The second objective of the athlete-leadership function is self-management. Self-management refers to managing one's mental, physical, and emotional state.

4.2.1 Managing one's mental state

Managing one's mental state means managing the neuro-structure of the brain and using neuroplasticity to adopt effective behaviors and habits in order to become a more effective servant-leader. Advancements in neuroscience have shown that individuals can change the neuro-structure of their brains by focusing their conscious thoughts purposefully and repeatedly to change behaviors and habits (Leaf 2013). This means that, when individuals focus their thoughts and mind repeatedly on adopting a new behavior or skill, the brain forms new neuropaths to automate the behavior or skill, making it a habit. The individual will then apply the behavior or skill unconsciously (without thinking about it). This process is called *neuroplasticity*. A leader should thus first understand how the brain functions before he or she attempts to manage it.

Research in neuroscience has revealed five general facts about the brain (Gunter 2013), and the acronym 'BRAIN' can be used to describe these:

- *Barcoded differently*: Each person's brain is 'wired' or 'barcoded' differently, which means that people receive and process information differently. The neuropaths in each person's brain are thus unique. This is important to know when interacting with others. People often assume that others think the same way they do, and with these assumptions come confusion, conflict, and miscommunication. Leaders should therefore understand that, when they communicate a message, others might interpret that message differently, because their neuro-structure is different. A leader should provide opportunities for reflection and questions after a message was communicated and be patient in addressing any miscommunication. A servant-leader understands that no two brains are alike, and therefore provides reflection time during conversations to ensure the information is processed accurately. A servant-leader also refers back to the other participants after a conversation, to ensure they understood the message correctly. A servant-leader, furthermore, listens to what is unsaid. He or she is attentive to body language and emotions, and attempts to understand the underlying message.

- **Roadmaps:** The second fact of the brain is that it forms 'roadmaps' or neuropaths. When attention and focus are given consistently and repeatedly to a particular thought in the conscious mind, the brain forms a new neuropath over time in order to apply the new skill or behavior effectively. For example, when a person learns to drive a motor vehicle for the first time, the conscious mind focuses most of its attention on mastering the skill of simultaneously operating the pedals, steering wheel, gearshift, and vehicle mirrors, while managing all external situations or scenarios. It takes repeated and consistent effort, focus, and training to master this skill over time. However, once a person has mastered the skill, he or she can drive and operate a vehicle without even thinking about it (unconsciously). This process of is called neuroplasticity, and it is a powerful way to use personal thoughts to build productive neuropaths (roadmaps) in the brain to ultimately become more effective in one's leadership behavior, approach, and habits.

- **Automation**: Once a new neuropath has formed, the brain locks it in the unconscious mind, enabling the person to apply the skill or behavior without much effort in the conscious mind. The brain thus aims continuously to automate behavior and skills, to become more effective and productive. Using the conscious mind takes energy. The brain therefore aims to automate behavior or skills by forming neuropaths in the conscious mind and then locking it into the unconscious mind. In this way, the brain spends less energy, and human functioning becomes more productive.

- **Impossible to delete old neuropaths**: Another fact of the brain is that it is almost impossible for the brain to delete or erase an old neuropath. The reason for this is that every time attention or focus in given to a neuropath in the conscious mind (thoughts), the neuropath is strengthened.

- **New neuropaths are more beneficial**: Instead of trying to erase old neuropaths, it is much easier and beneficial to create new neuropaths to change behavior or to adopt a new habit. An old neuropath will disintegrate over time as a person constantly uses the new neuropath. For example, it would be very difficult for a person to stop smoking when he or she constantly thinks about the satisfaction of smoking.

It will be much easier to quit smoking by adopting another, healthier habit and by focusing on the benefits of the new habit and its impact on oneself and others. It is thus important that leaders understand the process of how new behavior, skills, or habits are formed in the brain, to be able to change ineffective behavior or to attain new skills, with the aim of becoming a more effective leader.

One way to put neuroplasticity in action to change ineffective behavior is to use the **Thought Process Map** provided in Appendix A. This tool provides a step-by-step guide to forming new neuropaths over time. It includes five general steps to adopt a new behavior, and provides probing questions in each step to form new neuropaths.

Step 1 in changing a behavior or habit is to stop or pause when it is triggered by internal or external stimuli.

Step 2 of the Thought Process Map is to identify the reasons why one is behaving this way, by identifying any internal or external stimuli that trigger the unproductive behavior and to think about the negative outcomes, emotions, and consequences related to that behavior.

Step 3 of the Thought Process Map is to think about the new behavior one wants to adopt and clearly define it in a short sentence. The reasons why one wants to adopt this new behavior should be listed, as well as the positive outcomes and emotions associated with the new, more effective behavior. One can then draft an activation sentence — a statement — to trigger the new behavior in the future. The following format can be used to draft an activation sentence: *If ... happens, then I will do ... to achieve ..."* For example, let's say a person wants to lose weight, then an effective activation sentence might be: *If I crave chocolate, I will drink a cup of coffee instead, to achieve my goal of losing five pounds.*

Step 4 of the Thought Process Map is to visualize success. Athletes often visualize how they win a race. This visualization technique is powerful, as the brain cannot necessarily distinguish between reality and fiction. For example, what will happen when someone who was in a traumatic motor accident is asked to close his or her eyes and think intensively about the event and to re-imagine it in his or her mind? That person's heart rate will most probably increase and his or her hands might become sweaty. In other words, the person's body will start to react negatively, although the accident is only in his or her memory. Athletes often manipulate this process to prepare their minds and bodies before an event. Leaders can do the same, visualizing success to adopt new behaviors. The new neuropath is used and strengthened in the brain every time a person visualizes success, which means the body will respond much quicker in real life when the behavior is needed. A person should therefore visualize intensively that he or she is successfully executing the new behavior. During this visualization process, a person must include all senses and identify and write down the specific images, sounds, and emotions that come to mind. As this new neuropath is strengthened over time and with use, it is important to do this repeatedly and consistently over time.

Step 5 of the Thought Process Map is to list one to three actions to adopt the new behavior. For example, to exercise 2 times a week for 1 hour to lose 5 pounds in 11 weeks. These actions should be practical, measurable, and simple. Try not to list more than three actions, as it might be difficult to remember all of them in the future, and keep the actions succinct.

Once the Thought Process Map has been complete, one needs to review it regularly, because new neuropaths are formed with repetitive and consistent focus over time. A leader should thus review all steps of his or her Thought Process Map at least 10 minutes per day for 21 days to achieve sustainable results. The actions listed on the Thought Process Map should also be applied daily, until the new behavior becomes automated.

4.2.2   Managing one's physical state

Another dimension of self-management is managing one's physical state of energy and wellbeing. A person can have all the talents, skills, and knowledge, but without energy, a person is unable to deploy that talent, skill, and knowledge effectively to make a positive impact. It is like a Ferrari without gas. A Ferrari has wonderful power and torque, but, without gas, that power and torque cannot be activated, and the Ferrari is useless. The same applies to human energy. A person needs human energy to activate knowledge, skills, and natural talents to achieve a higher-purpose vision. It is therefore important that leaders manage their energy level, as this is the vehicle by which skill, knowledge, and talent are deployed. There are three ways in which human energy levels can be managed, namely (1) work–life balance, (2) a healthy diet and lifestyle, and (3) enhanced fitness.

Work–life balance refers to a balanced life in terms of work, relationships (family and friends), spirituality, health and fitness, recreation and fun, and personal growth. Activities in the domains of work, personal growth, and health and fitness will generally drain physical or mental energy, whereas activities in the domains of spirituality, recreation and fun, and relationships might generate new energy. The aim should thus be to have a balance across all domains. Work–life balance does not necessarily mean that one should have balance in terms of time, as this is not always feasible in our modern world of work and life. Work–life balance should rather be measured in terms of energy level and life satisfaction.

Leaders should evaluate their energy and life satisfaction regularly to identify any improvements across the six domains. Personal intervention should then be applied to address any imbalances. The Work–Life Satisfaction Wheel, presented in Appendix A, is useful for evaluating one's current work–life satisfaction levels in terms of spirituality, career, relationships, recreation and fun, health and fitness, and personal growth. Each dimension is given a satisfaction score of between 0 and 10 (*0 = Highly dissatisfied* and *10 = Highly satisfied*), which is plotted with a dot on the Work–Life Satisfaction Wheel. Once a score out of 10 has been allocated to each dimension, all the dots are connected to form a wheel. The connected dots forming a perfect circle indicates balance across the six life domains, while an imperfect circle indicates imbalance. The percentage of energy-draining activities (career, personal growth, and health and fitness) and energy-giving activities (spirituality, relationships, and recreation and fun) can also be calculated. This calculation will reveal the balance between energy-takers and energy-givers. Refer to the Work–Life Satisfaction Wheel in Appendix A to do this calculation.

Once a person has completed the Work–Life Satisfaction Wheel and reflected on the results, he or she needs to implement a plan of action to improve his or her work–life balance, especially if the energy-taking activities outweigh the energy-giving activities. These actions should be specific, realistic, and practical, with specific timelines. Balance across all six life dimensions will enhance holistic wellbeing in terms of spiritual health (spirituality), intellectual health (career and personal growth), physical health (health and fitness), and emotional health (relationships). In return, individuals will experience high energy.

A second way to enhance and maintain human energy is to improve one's diet and lifestyle. People often take better care of their vehicles than of their own bodies. They make sure they fill their vehicle with the right type of gas, check the oil regularly, and wash and service it regularly. Due to the complexity and speed of the modern world of work, people seem to eat fast, unhealthy food more often, fill their bodies with unhealthy substances such as alcohol, nicotine, and caffeine, and make fewer visits to the doctor or dentist for a check-up. We have only one body to live in for 70 to 100 years. The consumer mentality of modern human beings may have caused people to treat their bodies like any other consumable product, forgetting that it is irreplaceable. Leaders should therefore take care of their physical health and fitness to ensure they have the sustained energy levels needed to make a long-lasting positive impact on people, business, and society. Leaders should also encourage others to maintain a healthy lifestyle and diet.

A third way to improve one's energy levels is to enhance one's personal fitness. A fitter body produces positive results, physically and mentally. Regular exercise also helps to reduce stress levels and is an excellent coping mechanism. The brain releases endorphins in the body when a person exercises, which then improve emotional health. It is important to make exercise fun and to participate in physical activities that are enjoyable. Exercise should be a daily routine and something to look forward to. It would be very difficult to sustain a healthy exercise routine if the activities are unpleasant. A person's brain will then link negative emotions to the exercise, making it impossible to sustain the habit. However, if positive emotions are linked to exercise activities, positive emotions will drive a person to exercise again. In this way, the habit will become increasingly sustainable over time.

4.2.3 Managing one's emotional state

A third dimension of self-management is to manage one's emotional state. The ability to manage one's emotional state is called *emotional intelligence*, which can be defined as the skill to (a) perceive and express emotions effectively, (b) develop and maintain relationships, (c) cope with difficult or challenging situations or circumstances, and to (d) use emotions constructively (Stein & Book 2011). Emotional intelligence differs from intellectual intelligence, cognitive ability, general ability, and personality. It is a skill that can be learned.

Emotional intelligence consists of five broad dimensions, namely (1) self-perception, (2) self-expression, (3) interpersonal relationships, (4) decision-making, and (5) stress management (Stein & Book 2011). Self-perception refers to the skill of identifying one's strengths and weaknesses, to align one's strengths to a meaningful purpose, and to be aware of one's emotions. Self-perception thus includes three sub-dimensions, namely a healthy self-regard, self-actualization, and self-awareness.

The second dimension of emotional intelligence is self-expression, which refers to the skill to authentically express one's emotions in a diplomatic and constructive manner. Self-expression includes the sub-dimensions of constructive self-expression, assertiveness, and independence.

The third dimension of emotional intelligence is interpersonal relationships. This refers to the ability to build effective relationships with others, to understand and appreciate others, and to make a positive difference in others and society. Interpersonal relationships require good interpersonal skills, high empathy, and high social responsibility.

Decision-making is the fourth dimension of emotional intelligence, and can be defined as the skill to use emotions effectively to make good decisions. Decision-making includes three sub-dimensions, namely good problem-solving skills, high reality checking, and good impulse control.

The fifth dimension of emotional intelligence is stress management, which includes a high level of flexibility, stress tolerance, and optimism. The dimension of stress management can be defined as the skill to be resilient in difficult circumstances or situations, to be adaptable, and to remain positive in difficult situations.

Research has indicated that emotional intelligence becomes more important than technical ability in higher-level positions (Goleman 2004). This makes sense, as leaders are more involved with people. They need to spend more time building relationships with a variety of stakeholders and less time on technical tasks. Leaders also need the ability to cope in difficult situations and to master their emotions to make good decisions.

Leaders therefore need a high level of emotional intelligence to (a) identify their strengths and weaknesses, (b) apply their strengths and talents meaningfully to achieve a higher-purpose vision, (c) be authentic and express their emotions, (d) maintain good relationships and serve multiple stakeholders, (e) solve problems effectively, (d) make wise decisions, and (e) cope well in difficult situations or circumstances.

Leaders should evaluate their level of emotional intelligence regularly. This will help them identify any development areas and compile personal development actions to enhance their levels of emotional intelligence and become more effective leaders. There are several emotional intelligence assessments available in the market. One valuable assessment is the EQ-i 2.0 developed by MHS Assessments (https://tap.mhs.com/EQi20.asp). It also provides a 360-degree assessment option, in which a leader could ask others to evaluate his or her leadership behavior.

4.3 Self-improvement

The third objective of the athlete-leadership function is continuous self-improvement. Once a leader has identified his or her personal development areas in terms of values, leader-heart style, personality, cognitive ability, emotional intelligence, servant leadership attributes and competencies, or any trait or skill, a leader should compile a Personal Development Plan with specific actions and interventions aimed at becoming more effective.

The first step in personal development is to establish a Personal Career Plan, which is a written strategy that lists the next and ideal positions of a leader, in accordance with his or her life purpose and personal talents. The Personal Career Plan should include a skills and behavioral gap analysis to be successful in the next and ideal position.

A Career Plan Application Tool is provided in Appendix A. It first provides general questions to clarify a person's life purpose, and then presents a series of specific questions to determine how a current position aligns to the life purpose of an individual, the higher purpose of the organization, and the knowledge, skills, attributes, and talents of the individual. The third section of this application tool provides an opportunity to craft a job that is better aligned to the person's life purpose, knowledge, skills, attributes, and talents. The fourth section focuses on determining the ideal future position for an individual, in line with that person's life purpose, knowledge, skills, attributes, and talents. A gap analysis is also done in this section, to determine the type of knowledge, skills, and attributes the individual still needs to be successful in the future ideal position. In the fifth section of the Career Plan Application Tool, the individual's current, next, and future positions are listed.

The second phase in personal development is to compile a Personal Development Plan. A guide to this is provided in Appendix A. In the first section of this application tool, the individual's career path is indicated, in alignment with the individual's career plan. Thereafter, the person's knowledge, skills, abilities, and attribute gaps for his or her current and future positions (as per the Career Plan) are listed, together with suggested learning activities to close those gaps. Learning activities can be clustered into foundational learning activities, experiential learning activities, and personal learning activities. Foundational learning activities are those activities that enhance knowledge, such as formal classroom training, educational qualifications, electronic learning, seminars, webinars, conferences, workshops, group learning, research, and reading. Experiential learning activities are activities that improve competence, such as on-the-job training, simulations, gamification, action learning, and workplace assignments. Personal learning refers to activities that create personal transformation, such as coaching, mentoring, social learning, and reflection. It is important to include foundational, experiential, and personal learning activities in a personal development plan, as this is the most sustainable way to gain new knowledge, skills, and behaviors. In the last section of the Personal Development Plan, learning activities are prioritized and specific outcomes and target dates are planned for each learning activity.

4.4 Self-revelation

Self-revelation refers to being and showing one's true self. This objective is underpinned by four principles, namely to (1) discover and apply personal uniqueness, (2) identify and bridge personal weaknesses, (3) communicate openly and honestly, and to (4) be consistent and transparent.

4.4.1   Discover and apply personal uniqueness

The first principle of self-revelation is to discover one's uniqueness, in other words, to discover one's unique talents, attributes, and skills. People often compare themselves to others or aim to become like someone else, without considering the beauty and wonder of their own uniqueness. Each person is beautifully and wonderfully made and has a unique life purpose and set of talents, attributes, and skills. It is this uniqueness that matters.

Individuals can discover their uniqueness by completing different psychometric assessments and by asking close friends and family to identify personal talents, attributes, and skills. Past successes could also reveal a person's unique talents and skills. Self-reflection plays a major role in this process of understanding one's uniqueness and how it could benefit others. Once a person has discovered his or her uniqueness, he or she needs to develop and apply it. This means that a person should align his or her uniqueness to a life purpose and a career. Individuals should also continuously strive to improve their unique talents, attributes, and skills to make a positive difference in people, organizations, and society.

4.4.2   Identify and bridge personal weaknesses

The second principle of self-revealing is to identify and bridge weaknesses. A leader should be confident and humble enough to identify personal weaknesses, communicate it to others, and to then align the strengths of others to those weaknesses. In this way, the probability of success is greater. If a leader fails to communicate a weakness, the success of a team or an organization could be in jeopardy.

An organization or team functions like a human body. All parts in the human body are required for the body to function optimally. Each part in the human body is also unique, and one cannot fulfil the role of the other, and when one part suffers, the whole body suffers. The same applies to people in an organization or a team. People should acknowledge and respect their own and others' uniqueness, and not try to fulfil the role of others or expect others to fulfil their role. People who work together must understand each other's weaknesses and strengths to function optimally. It is thus important to understand personal weaknesses, to communicate these to others, and to bridge personal weaknesses with the strengths of others. This will ultimately ensure that the team or organization functions optimally.

4.4.3 Communicate openly and honestly

The third principle of self-revelation is to communicate openly and honestly. Trust is a crucial component in any relationship, including work relationships, and communication can break or create trust. For example, employees' trust in the leader will increase when the leader honestly and openly communicates to employees that the organization is experiencing financial difficulties and how employees can assist to address this challenge. In this case, the probability of overcoming those challenges will be greater. However, when the leader withholds important information from employees and communicates a vague and dishonest message to them, employees' trust in the leader will decrease, which will influence their commitment and engagement levels in the organization, which will ultimately reduce the probability of the organization overcoming the challenge. It is therefore important that leaders are honest and open when they communicate a message to others.

One way to ensure one's communication is open and honest is to use the 'TRUTH' method to validate a message, namely:

- *True facts*: Ensure the message reflects the true facts.
- *Relevant facts*: Ensure the message includes all the relevant facts.
- *Uncertainty*: Ensure the message addresses any form of uncertainty.
- *Time*: Ensure the message is communicated at the right time.
- *Helpful*: Ensure the message is helpful to others.

4.4.4 Be consistent and transparent

The fourth principle of self-revelation is to be consistent and transparent. This means that leaders should be consistent and reliable in their daily behavior and share their thoughts openly with others, but in a constructive manner. When a leader behaves inconsistently, others lose respect for and trust in the leader. Leaders can only be consistent when they are revealing their true self. Inconsistent behavior or performance often happens when people (a) are not true to themselves, (b) pretend to be like someone else, or they (c) want to do something that is not in line with their unique potential, talent, knowledge, and skills. Hence, the best way to be consistent and reliable is to be one's true self and to apply one's uniqueness.

Leaders should also be transparent and share their thoughts openly. Strategic or project failure often results from people not sharing their emotions and thoughts, perhaps because they did not have the opportunity to do so. A servant-leader should thus create an environment in which each person feels safe and secure to share his or her thoughts and emotions. An environment that encourages the sharing of thoughts will (a) enhance knowledge sharing, (b) ensure better decision-making, and (c) ensure higher commitment levels from all involved. It is important to share one's thoughts and emotions in a constructive manner, in other words, in a manner that uplifts the other person. Leaders should never communicate their thoughts or emotions to manipulate or force their will on others. This is not the purpose of being transparent. The purpose of transparency is to encourage shared knowledge, better decision-making, and higher commitment. A leader should thus also encourage others to share their thoughts and emotions in a constructive manner that uplifts all members of the team.

4.5 Self-reflection

The fifth objective of the athlete-leadership function is to self-reflect regularly. Effective self-reflection includes four general principles, namely: (1) clear purpose, (2) specific outcomes, (3) solitude, and (4) intentional focus.

4.5.1 Clear purpose

Self-reflection should be intentional and have a clear purpose. Leaders should schedule self-reflection time well in advance and clearly define the purpose of a self-reflection session. General reasons for self-reflection might include personal development, generating insights from past behavior, discovering personal strengths and development areas, making decisions, or planning for the future.

4.5.2   Specific outcomes

Once the purpose of a self-reflection session has been defined, a leader should specify the outcomes he or she wants to achieve during the session. For example, a leader might want to self-reflect to evaluate the impact of his or her behavior on the commitment levels of others (purpose) and because he or she wants to adopt a better way to improve the commitment levels of his or her team (outcome). Specifying the outcome prior to a self-reflection session will enhance the effectiveness of the session and make it more valuable. It will also encourage the leader to generate specific actions to be implemented after the session.

4.5.3   Experience solitude

The third principle of self-reflection is to experience solitude. Reflection is a mental process that requires focus and concentration. Distractions, noise, people, and technology should thus be avoided during a reflection session. The best way to reflect is to take oneself out of the current environment or situation and find a quiet place to think, where there are no distractions or noise. It should also be a place that induces calmness.

4.5.4   Intentional focus

The fourth principle of effective reflection is intentional focus. Self-reflection cannot happen without focus. A leader should thus determine specific topics or areas to focus on in a reflection session. For example, a leader might want to self-reflect to evaluate the impact of his or her behavior on the commitment levels of others (purpose) and consider adopting a better way to improve the commitment levels of his or her team (outcome) by focusing specifically on his or her communication style in stressful situations (focus point).

A Self-reflection Guide is provided in Appendix A that could help a leader to plan and implement self-reflection sessions effectively. This Guide provides several questions to assist a leader to establish an intention statement prior to a reflection session. An intention statement describes the purpose, outcome(s), place, date, time, and focus areas of a self-reflection session.

The Self-reflection Guide also provides a step-by-step process containing the activities to perform during a self-reflection session. The first step in a reflection session is to review the purpose and outcome of the session, in order to understand the context. In the second step, the leader needs approximately 10–20 minutes to reflect on each focus area and to translate thoughts into inputs, reasons, actions, and outcomes. The Thought Process Map, discussed earlier in this chapter, might also be useful in this process, if the focus area is behavioral. During the reflection session, a leader should also think about past events, current patterns, and future scenarios related to the focus area and write down thoughts that come to mind. Thereafter, the leader should reflect on the desired behavior or outcome and visualize success. The third step during the reflection session is to add more detail to one's written notes and summarize the outcome of the self-reflection in one sentence. This will make it easier to remember it afterwards. In the fourth step, the leader should compare the outcome of a reflection session with the desired outcome listed in the intention statement. If the desired outcome was not reached, a person should repeat the previous steps (Steps 1–3). In the final step, the leader compiles and prioritizes actions to improve, together with specific timelines and measures. After the reflection session, the leader implements the actions, measures its success, and plans the next self-reflection session.

4.6 Stay within the rules

The final objective of the athlete-leadership function is to always stay within the rules. Staying within the rules means practicing good business ethics and abiding by relevant laws, regulations, rules, and policies. A servant-leader always operates within the law and conducts business ethically. A servant-leader knows that unethical behavior comes to light over time and that it will have destructive consequences for him or her, as well as others. History is full of the negative consequences of unethical and immoral leadership, and shows how these destructive consequences often outlive the leader. It is thus important that leaders (a) understand the 'rules of the game' (i.e. relevant legislation, regulations, rules, and policies), (b) stay informed on any amendments, (c) operate well within the rules, (d) encourage others to adhere to the rules, and (e) reward ethical behavior and discipline unethical behavior.

Sometimes, the rules are unethical and immoral. What should a leader then do? In those circumstances, the leader should consult all relevant stakeholders (customers, employees, the organization, suppliers, and society, with consideration of the environment) to determine the action that would produce the best moral benefit for all. A leader should then stand up for what is right by challenging the unethical rule at a higher authority.

4.7 The characteristics and competencies of the athlete-leadership function

The characteristics required to be effective in the athlete-leadership function are: authenticity, humility, and integrity. Authenticity can be described as (a) showing one's true identity, intentions, and motivations, (b) being true to oneself, (c) being open to learning from criticism, (d) being transparent, and (e) showing consistent behavior. Humility can be defined as being (a) stable and modest, (b) self-aware of personal strengths and development areas, and (c) open to new learning opportunities, while (d) perceiving personal talents and achievements in the right perspective, (e) valuing and activating the talent of others, (f) enjoying helping others succeed, and (g) giving credit to others for successful completion of a task. Integrity refers to having strong moral principles and being honest, fair, and ethical in all circumstances. The traits of authenticity, humility, and integrity will collectively assist a leader to apply the principles of self-knowledge, self-management, self-improvement, self-revelation, self-reflection, and staying within the rules.

It will thus be difficult to apply the principles of the athlete-leadership function if a leader lacks one or more of these traits. For example, it will be very difficult for a leader to stay within the rules if he or she does not have a high level of integrity. Similarly, leaders will struggle to manage or improve themselves if they do not have humility. It will furthermore be hard to reveal one's true self if one does not possess a high level of authenticity. A leader should thus regularly evaluate his or her personal levels of authenticity, humility, and integrity and reflect on the results, in order to implement the necessary personal development interventions to become a more effective servant-leader.

The competency associated with the athlete-leadership function is personal capability. Personal capability refers to the ability to manage and develop oneself towards enhanced (a) personal effectiveness, (b) wellbeing, and (c) optimal functioning. The main objective of the athlete-leadership function is to develop oneself to become a role model for others and an ambassador for the higher-purpose vision. Leaders therefore need to be able to lead themselves effectively before they can lead others.

PART 3

THE HANDS OF A SERVANT-LEADER

(OPERATIONAL SERVANT LEADERSHIP)

The *heart* dimension of servant leadership was discussed in Part 1 of this book, and the *head* dimension was discussed in Part 2. In this part, the *hands* dimension of servant leadership is discussed, which refers to operational servant leadership. Two servant-leadership functions are part of operational servant leadership, namely the steward-leadership function and the farmer-leadership function. These functions are discussed in detail in Chapters 5 and 6, and practical guidelines are provided to apply these functions in an organization.

Before a servant-leader can apply operational servant leadership, he or she needs to invert the hierarchy. Inverting the hierarchy means a leader puts the customer and employees first. If a leader does not invert the hierarchy, employees will serve leaders, and customers and society will suffer. The only way an organization can function optimally is when leaders serve employees and employees serve customers, because employees are closest to producing the product and to serving the customers, and the customers and society are the reason why an organization exists.

Leaders must therefore set a higher-purpose vison for the organization, one that serves multiple stakeholders, by applying strategic servant leadership and then invert the hierarchy to apply operational servant leadership to serve and empower employees to achieve the higher-purpose vision. Leaders should thus apply the soldier-leadership function first, to set, translate, and execute a higher-purpose vision, and then apply the athlete-leadership function to become role models and ambassadors for the higher-purpose vision. Thereafter, leaders must invert the hierarchy and apply the farmer- and steward-leadership functions to align, care for, and grow employees and to continuously monitor and improve. During operational servant leadership, the leader will use the Capability and Capacity Frameworks of the company (which were developed during the soldier-leadership function, when the higher-purpose vision was translated) to align, care for, and grow employees, and also use the processes, systems, and policies of the company (which were also developed during the soldier-leadership function, when the higher-purpose vision was translated) to monitor performance and progress in achieving the higher-purpose vision and to continuously improve. The process of inverting the hierarchy is presented in Figure 4, below.

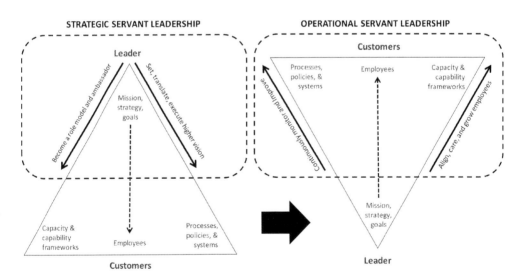

Figure 4. The process of inverting the hierarchy

CHAPTER 5
THE STEWARD-LEADERSHIP FUNCTION

The third function of a servant-leader is to continuously monitor and improve. This function falls within the operational servant-leadership domain. A steward is used as an analogy to explain the objectives and principles of this function.

A steward is someone who manages the belongings of others effectively, to produce a return for the owner. A good steward is someone who acknowledges that he or she is not the owner, but a steward, and aims to produce the best return for the owner in the shortest time span. Stewards have a 'give' mentality, and use their talents, finances, position, resources, and assets to produce a return that is beneficial for others.

Good stewards consider both time and return, and know that all things in life have a start and an end. For example, all people have a birth date and death date. The same is true for positional power, financial wealth, knowledge, skills, and talents. All things in life have an expiry date. People are often aware of the start date, but the end date of things are not always known. For example, people do not know the day of their death or the day when they will lose their financial wealth, or even when they will lose their knowledge, skill, or ability due to age, sickness, or accident. Only the state of things in the present time is known. A steward focuses on and operates in the present while reflecting on the past and taking cognizance of the future.

A key principle of stewardship is thus to use what was loaned to you to produce the best return for others in the present time, with a conscious awareness of the unknown future. Some people can produce the same or even better return in the same timeframe. This is good stewardship. Stewards use all things wisely to produce the best possible return to the benefit of others.

The same principles apply to leadership. An effective leader will use the company's finances, resources, assets, and his or her leadership position, knowledge, talents, skills, and abilities to produce the greatest return, to the benefit of the organization and other people. Effective leaders will also manage their personal wealth, relationships, assets, and attributes well, to produce a beneficial outcome for others. Good leaders have a steward life-perspective, rather than an owner life-perspective.

Servant-leaders accept a leadership position, not to gain more power to achieve selfish objectives, but to make a positive difference in the world and to leave a long-lasting positive legacy in people and society. They use their knowledge, talents, and skills to create value for others in the world. The intent of a servant-leader originates from a loving heart, and the intent is to use all things, position, and abilities to empower people, to build sustainable and high-performing organizations, and to create a humane society.

Another principle of stewardship is monitoring progress and initiating continuous improvement. Once a leader has set a higher-purpose vision for an organization and translated that vision into a mission, strategy, and employee goals, the leader must continuously monitor performance against those goals and partner with employees to achieve the goals. The leader should also aim to continuously improve the company's products, services, business processes, systems, and policies, to ensure their relevance and applicability to the present and future context. Without continuous improvement, an organization will become irrelevant.

The characteristic required to practice good stewardship is accountability, and the competency associated with the steward-leadership function is stewardship. Accountability can be defined as (a) being responsible by (b) monitoring performance continuously, by (c) setting clear expectations in accordance with one's capability and life purpose, and by (d) holding others accountable. The competency of Stewardship refers to (a) the ability to look after the common interests of society, an organization, and other people, with (b) the intent to leave a positive and sustainable legacy in the world, and with (c) a life perspective of being a caretaker, rather than an owner. Without the trait of accountability and the skill of stewardship, it would be very difficult to be a good steward.

The objectives, characteristic, and competency of the steward-leadership role are summarized in Table 10.

Table 10. The objectives, characteristic, and competency of the steward-leadership function (Coetzer et al. 2017)

Function	Continuously monitor and improve
Leadership question	Who is the owner?
Objectives	• Good stewardship • Monitor performance and progress • Improve products, processes, systems, policies, and procedures
Characteristics	• Accountability
Competency	• Stewardship

5.1 Good stewardship

The first objective of the steward-leadership function is to apply good stewardship. Stewardship can be divided into personal and employment stewardship.

5.1.1 Personal stewardship

Personal stewardship refers to managing one's lifetime, life roles, finances, resources, assets, knowledge, skills, and natural talents in such a way to produce a beneficial return for others. Lifetime is the time one is given on earth, and life roles refer to specific roles or positions, such as being a father, mother, brother, sister, friend, child, or spouse. Finances, resources, and assets are personal money and possessions. Knowledge, skills, and natural abilities refer to a person's educational qualifications and abilities to perform a certain task or activity. Good stewards use their lifetime, life roles, finances, resources, assets, knowledge, skills, and natural talents effectively to produce the greatest return for others in the shortest time span.

Personal stewardship should be planned; it does not happen by chance. Table 11 provides a structure for compiling a Personal Stewardship Plan. The first step in compiling this Plan is to reflect on the type of return one has provided for others to date. This can be done in the first four columns of Table 11. The second step is to plan how one will achieve a future desired return on one's lifetime, talents, life roles, finances, resources, and assets, to produce a return for others. This is done in columns five and six of Table 11.

Table 11. Personal Stewardship Plan Template

Factor	Alpha	Current return	Omega	Future return	Omega
Time (Lifetime)	*Start date*		*Today's date*		*Future date*
Talents	*Start date*		*Today's date*		*Future date*
Position (life roles)	*Start date*		*Today's date*		*Future date*
Finances	*Start date*		*Today's date*		*Future date*
Resources/Assets	*Start date*		*Today's date*		*Future date*

The first column in Table 11 lists the different stewardship dimensions, which are your lifetime, talents, life roles, finances, resources, and assets. In the second column, the start date of each stewardship dimension can be listed. For example, in the first row (*Lifetime*), your birthdate can be listed as a start date. In the second row (*Talents*), the date you discovered a new talent can be listed. In the third row (*Position/Life roles*), your marriage date can be listed as the start date when the life role of spouse was chosen, or the birthdate of a child could be listed as a start date when the life role of parent was chosen. In the fourth row (*Finances*), the date when you received your first income can be listed. In the fifth row (*Resources/Assets*), the date you received a resource or bought a new asset can be listed.

Once the start dates have been listed, one can initiate the first step in compiling a Personal Stewardship Plan, namely to determine a present (or current) return. A present (or current) return is the return one produced for others by using one's lifetime, talents, life positions, finances, resources, and assets from the start date to the present date. The third column (*Current return*) in Table 11 can be used to note a current return. The first *Omega* date (fourth column) is therefore the present date. This is the first *Omega* check-in date — when one reflects back on how one's lifetime, talents, life roles, finances, resources, and assets were used to date to produce a return for others.

The following questions might help to determine a present or current return:

- What returns have you provided to others with the lifetime given to date?
- What returns have you provided to others in using your talents to date?
- What returns have you provided to date as a parent, child, brother, sister, or friend?
- What returns have you provided to date using your personal finances?
- What returns have you provided to date using personal resources or assets?

Once you have reflected on the past return, you can use the fifth column (*Future return*) to plan a desired future return. A future return is that which you want to produce for others in the future, using your lifetime, talents, life roles, finances, resources, and assets. The next *Omega* check-in date is the (future) date when you want to deliver the return. This planned date can be noted in the sixth column (the second *Omega* date) in Table 11.

The following questions might help to plan a future return:

- If you are given five additional years of lifetime, what return would you like to give to others?
- In the next five years, what return would you like to give to others, using your talents?
- In the next five years, what return would you like to give as a spouse, parent, child, brother, sister, or friend?
- In the next five years, what return would you like to give using your personal finances?
- In the next five years, what return would you like to give using your personal resources or assets?

Once a Personal Stewardship Plan has been compiled, specific actions should be listed to implement the plan. Regular (*Omega*) check-in dates should be scheduled to reflect on the planned return versus the achieved return. One should also request regular feedback from others, to determine whether a positive and long-lasting return was produced to the benefit of others and society.

5.1.2 Employment stewardship

Employment stewardship works on the same principle, and refers to the return a person produces during a time of employment, whether self-employed or employed by a company. The factors included in an Employment Stewardship Plan are (a) employment time, (b) talents, knowledge, skills, and ability, (c) employment position, (d) company finances, and (e) company resources or assets. Employment time is the duration of employment at an employer or the duration of being self-employed. Talents, knowledge, skills, and abilities are the specific education, competencies, and attributes a person applies in the workplace to produce a return for multiple stakeholders in the company. Employment position is the job title or position a person holds in an organization and the type of work a person performs. The finances, resources, and assets are the company's budget, resources, and assets that were allocated to a person during employment.

A good steward manages the finances, resources, and assets of a company well and uses his or her employment time, talents, knowledge, skills, and abilities effectively during employment, to produce the best return for the company and its employees, customers, shareholders, and suppliers. An exceptional steward produces a greater return in a shorter time span. A template for compiling an Employment Stewardship Plan is provided in Table 12.

Table 12. Template for an Employment Stewardship Plan

Factor	Alpha	Current return	Omega	Future return	Omega
Time (Employment)	*Start date*		*Today's date*		*Future date*
Talents	*Start date*		*Today's date*		*Future date*
Position	*Start date*		*Today's date*		*Future date*
Finances	*Start date*		*Today's date*		*Future date*
Resources/Assets	*Start date*		*Today's date*		*Future date*

The first step is to reflect on the type of return you have provided for multiple stakeholders during your employment, to date. The first four columns of Table 12 can be used to list a current return for each stewardship dimension. The start dates of each stewardship dimension can be listed in the second column (*Alpha* column). The return you have produced to date for each stewardship dimension can be summarized in the third column (*Current return*). The first *Omega* date is the present date, which can be noted in column four (first *Omega* column).

The following questions can be used to determine a present (or current) return:

- What return have you provided for the company and its customers, employees, shareholders, and suppliers during your employment period to date?
- What return have you provided to date for the company and its customers, employees, shareholders, and suppliers, using your talents, knowledge, or skills in your job?
- What return have you provided to date for the company and its customers, employees, shareholders, and suppliers in your current position?
- What return have you provided to date for the company and its customers, employees, shareholders, and suppliers in managing the company's finances?
- What return have you provided to date for the company and its customers, employees, shareholders, and suppliers in managing the company's resources and assets?

The answers to the abovementioned questions can be completed in the *Current return* column of the Employment Stewardship Plan (Table 12).

The second step in compiling an Employment Stewardship Plan is to plan a future desired return by determining how you will use your employment time, talents, position, and company finances, resources, and assets to produce a future return for the company and its stakeholders (customers, employees, shareholders, and suppliers). Columns five and six of Table 12 can be used to plan this future return.

In column five (*Future return*), you can note the type of return you want to produce in the future for each stewardship dimension, and, in the sixth column (second *Omega* column), the desired target date for each return.

The following questions can be used to plan a future return for each stewardship dimension:

- In the next five years, what return would you like to produce for the company and its customers, employees, shareholders, and suppliers in your current job?
- In the next five years, what return would you like to produce for the company and its customers, employees, shareholders, and suppliers using your talents, knowledge, and skills in your current position?
- In the next five years, what return would you like to produce for the company and its customers, employees, shareholders, and suppliers as a leader?
- In the next five years, what return would you like to produce for the company and its customers, employees, shareholders, and suppliers in managing the company's finances?
- In the next five years, what return would you like to produce for the company and its customers, employees, shareholders, and suppliers in managing the company's resources and assets?

The answers to the abovementioned questions can be listed in the *Future return* column of the Employment Stewardship Plan (Table 12). Once you have decided on an Employment Stewardship Plan, specific actions should be implemented to achieve the desired returns. Regular *Omega* check-ins and sessions should also be scheduled, to monitor your progress on achieving the desired returns.

Companies can incorporate these plans in recruitment and on-boarding processes by, for example, asking a new employee to compile an Employment Stewardship Plan. These plans can also be used in talent management and succession processes, to plan desired future returns after a person has been promoted to a higher position.

5.2 Monitor performance and progress continuously

The second objective of the steward-leadership function is to continuously monitor performance and progress. In the soldier-leadership function, the leader set a higher-purpose vision for the organization and translated that vision into a mission, strategy, and employee goals. In the steward-leadership function, the leader monitors performance and progress to ensure these goals are achieved.

5.2.1 Performance management frameworks

Leaders should focus on specific inputs during performance management, to ensure the right outputs are achieved. Over the past decade, researchers and practitioners have identified specific input factors required to sustain a high-performing organization. For example, in the 1990s, Kaplan and Norton (1992) introduced the Balanced Scorecard, which consists of four main factors to sustain high performance, namely (1) customer excellence, (2) continuous innovation, as well as learning and development, (3) simple and effective business processes, and (4) financial performance.

In 2001, another high-performance organizational model was introduced by Owen, Mundy, Guild, and Guild (2001), which included five input factors: (1) knowledge of market trends, (2) shared vision, mission, and values, (3) effective leadership practices, (4) effective employee behavior and attitude, and (5) an enabling infrastructure.

In 2006, Blanchard introduced a framework called the HPO SCORES Model. In this model, the input factors are (1) shared information and open communication, (2) compelling vision (purpose and values), (3) ongoing learning, (4) a relentless focus on customer results, (5) energizing systems and structures, and (6) shared power and high involvement (Blanchard 2010). The output factors of Blanchard's model are unleashed power and potential of employees, with the organization becoming a preferred employer, a preferred provider, and a preferred investment.

De Waal (2012) recently presented a model that includes five main input factors to sustain high performance in an organization, namely (1) quality leadership and management, (2) openness and action orientation, (3) long-term orientation, (4) continuous improvement and renewal, and (5) a quality workforce (employees). A detailed description of De Waal's (2012) five input factors are presented in Table 13.

Table 13. Input factors of a high-performing organization (De Waal 2012)

Quality management	Openness and action orientation	Long-term orientation	Continuous improvement and renewal	Quality workforce
• Trustful relationships • Managing with integrity • Action-oriented decision-making • Effective coaching • Enforcing accountability • Addressing poor performance actively • Strategy and values of the organization are known and complied with	• Regular interaction with employees • Allowing employees to take risks and make mistakes • Embracing change • Collective intelligence and knowledge-sharing • Maintaining a performance culture	• Building sustainable relationships and partnerships with internal and external stakeholders • Maintaining high levels of customer excellence • Creating a secure workplace for employees (job security and emotional availability) • Building managerial talent pipelines from within	• Extraordinary strategy • Simple and standardized processes • Ensuring all performance parameters are reported regularly • Continuous improvement of products or services	• Holding employees accountable for performance • Flexible workforce and management structure • Continuously improving the competence of employees

A consolidation of the four models or frameworks to sustain a high-performing organization are provided on a timeline in Table 14. Similar themes across the four frameworks are listed in the first column, namely (1) financial performance, (2) customer satisfaction, (3) a higher-purpose vision, (4) adequate and effective business processes and systems, (5) continuous improvement, (6) competent employees, (7) leadership effectiveness, (8) engaged employees, (9) and authentic and regular communication.

It is important to note that a shift in focus of the models is evident over the years, from financial performance in earlier years (1992) to leadership effectiveness, employee engagement, and authentic communication in recent years (2006 and 2012). Financial performance is now considered an output, not an input. Leaders should focus primarily on the input factors, such as customer satisfaction, a higher-purpose vision, adequate and effective business processes and systems, continuous improvement, competent and engaged employees, leadership effectiveness, and authentic communication, to sustain a high-performing organization. Only then can an organization expect the output of sustainable financial performance.

Table 14. Consolidation of the input factors to sustain a high-performing organization

FOCUS	Kaplan & Norton (1992)	Owen, Mundy, Guild, & Guild (2001)	Blanchard (2006)	De Waal (2012)
Financial performance	Finance			
Customer satisfaction	Customer	Knowledge of market	Focus on customer	Long-term orientation
Higher-purpose vision	Vision & strategy	Shared vision	Compelling vision	Continuous improvement
Business processes and systems	Business processes	Enabling infrastructure	Energizing systems	Continuous improvement
Continuous improvement	Innovation		Organizational capability	Renewal
Competent employees	Learning		Ongoing learning	Workforce quality
Leadership effectiveness		Leadership practices	Shared power	Management quality
Engaged employees		Employee behavior	High involvement	Workforce quality
Authentic communication			Shared info	Openness

Once a higher-purpose vision has been set and translated, leaders must spend most of their time (approximately 70%) on (1) improving customer service, (2) enhancing the competence and engagement levels of employees, and (3) standardizing and simplifying business processes and systems. Leaders must improve customer service by continuously identifying the needs of customers and society and then improving the organization's products and services to meet those needs. Leaders should, furthermore, improve the quality of the products and services of an organization and continuously strive to reduce costs. In this way, customers will receive better-quality products and services at lower prices, in line with their specific needs. Leaders should also ensure that more customers experience the value of the organization's products and services, in other words, that the quantity of customers increases.

The second focus area of leaders should be to enhance the competence and engagement levels of employees, because employees are closest to the production of the product and to serving the customer. Enhancing the competence levels of employees refers to continuously improving their level of knowledge, skill, and ability while activating the true potential and natural talents of individuals. This can be done by measuring individuals' competence against their work goals and developing a Personal Development Plan with employees. This Plan should include foundational, experiential, and personal training activities. Employee engagement refers to the level of energy and motivation an employee experiences in performing work tasks. Employees may be competent to complete a task, but if they lack the required energy or motivation, they will not be able to apply their competence effectively. It is thus important to continuously measure employees' levels of energy and motivation to complete tasks. Practical ways of measuring the energy, competence, and motivation levels of employees are provided in Chapter 6.

Leaders should, thirdly, focus on standardizing and simplifying business processes and systems in the organization. During the soldier-leadership function, business processes and systems were aligned in support of the higher-purpose vision, mission, and strategy of the company. In the steward-leadership function, these processes and systems should be improved continuously to enhance productivity and effectiveness. The general aim of improving business processes and systems is to standardize and simplify these throughout the organization. Both standardization and simplification will increase effectiveness and productivity, which will enable the delivery of higher-quality products and services at a better price and within a shorter time frame. Standardization and simplification of business processes and systems will, in addition, decrease the work demands employees experience, which will increase their effectiveness, which, in turn, will enable them to render exceptional customer service.

Several outcomes can be expected when leaders focus on improving customers' satisfaction, employee competence and engagement, and business processes and systems. For example, when high-quality products and services are offered to customers at reduced prices, general customer satisfaction will increase. When customer satisfaction increases, customers will continue to buy from the company, and will also refer the company's products and services to family, friends, and colleagues. Customers thus become ambassadors for the company's products and services, resulting in more products and services being sold to more people.

Hence, when a leader focuses on (a) enhancing the quality of a product, (b) reducing the cost of a product, and on (c) selling the product to more customers, the company will generate a higher and sustainable income. When the leader focuses on enhancing the competence, energy, and motivation levels of employees, employees are more capable of delivering on work-related goals and rendering exceptional customer service. When business processes and systems are standardized and simplified, the overall effectiveness of the organization increases. More effective processes and systems also improve the engagement levels of employees, as these reduce the work demands employees experience in completing their work. This will improve customer satisfaction, as products and services can now be of a higher quality, at a lower cost, delivered within a shorter time frame.

The inputs of quality, cost, and quantity will thus generate the output of sustainable income. The inputs of employee competence, energy, and motivation will generate an outcome of sustainable delivery, and the inputs of standardized and simplified processes and systems will generate an outcome of enhanced effectiveness. Higher income, delivery, and effectiveness will increase general organizational performance and impact.

Although leaders should mainly focus on monitoring and improving the abovementioned inputs to sustain a high-performing organization, leaders should still measure the outcomes of income, delivery, and effectiveness. However, these outcomes should only be measured 20% of the time, for example, quarterly. The overall outcome of organizational performance and impact in line with the higher-purpose vision, mission, and strategy should be measured approximately 10% of the time, for example annually or bi-annually. The inputs, however, should be measured about 70% of the time, so, daily or weekly. Figure 5 summarizes the focus areas in sustaining a high-performing organization in terms of the required inputs and outputs.

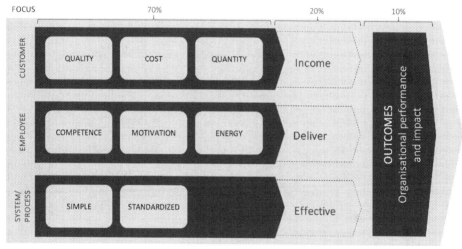

Figure 5. Performance focus areas in terms of
organizational inputs and outputs

Organizational outcomes should not only be measured in terms of performance, but also in terms of impact. Many organizations only measure their performance in terms of single-stakeholder value, such as financial performance or shareholder return, but fail to measure impact on customers, employees, society, and the environment. Often, organizations showed good performance in terms of financial performance and shareholder value, but failed to deliver a positive impact in any of the other areas. It is important that leaders monitor and measure the performance of the organization as well as the impact of the organization from a multiple-stakeholder perspective, which includes value creation for customers, employees, suppliers, shareholders, society, and the environment.

5.2.2 The performance management process

Many performance management systems, procedures, and policies are based on pride and fear. For example, companies will motivate employees with bonusses (money) or higher positions (status) to perform better, or will threaten employees with unemployment or disciplinary action to address poor performance. In such instances, companies rely on the greediness of mankind to perform better, or depend on the fear of individuals to correct poor performance. It is easy to identify when performance in a company is driven by pride or fear. For instance, talented employees in pride-driven organizations will only perform at their best when bonusses are paid or when they can attain a higher status in the organization. However, when the organization struggles financially due to unforeseen circumstances and cannot afford to pay bonusses or to promote employees, these employees leave the organization at a time when the organization needs them most. A performance management system based on fear or pride (greed) is therefore not sustainable.

Performance management systems, processes, and policies should rather be based on purpose and impact. When a company's higher-purpose vision is effectively translated into employee goals and those goals align well with the life purpose of individuals, employees will motivate themselves to perform, and their optimum performance will not be dependent on any external source of motivation. They will thus experience intrinsic motivation. Extrinsic motivational sources then become enablers to activate individual potential in line with a higher purpose, to ultimately create a positive, long-lasting, and sustainable impact for multiple stakeholders. When an employee's life purpose and interests align well with the higher-purpose vision, the reason to perform will be to achieve a meaningful outcome, not greed or the fear of unemployment.

A performance management system should therefore be based on two principles, namely love and purpose (not pride or fear). When love and purpose are at the heart of a performance management system, employees' performance is driven by the positive impact they create for others. However, if a performance management system is based on pride or fear, employees are driven by selfish motives and use the system for personal gain, to the detriment of the company and other stakeholders.

Organizations driven by love and purpose will also reward employees for making a long-lasting positive impact to the benefit of multiple stakeholders and encourage employees to activate their true talent and potential to achieve a meaningful life purpose.

It is for this reason that the first phase in any performance management process is to establish meaningful goals for employees, in line with the higher-purpose vision of the organization and with the higher life purpose of an employee. Goal setting should be done in consultation with the employee, and both the employee and the leader should agree on the goals. Employee goals should be specific, with measurable outcomes and timelines. Once the employee and the leader have agreed on a set of goals, a performance contract can be finalized. The second phase in the performance management process is to (a) focus on daily inputs to achieve the goal, (b) monitor progress, (c) provide regular feedback, and (d) provide continuous recognition and support. The third phase in the performance management process is to review the outcome.

The performance management process is similar to a sporting event such as a soccer, football, or rugby match. Before the game, the team and coach will agree on a game plan. Individual athletes and the coach will also agree on specific individual goals, in line with the overall game plan. The responsibility of the coach, in the first phase, is to (a) align individual talent to a set of goals according to the higher-purpose game plan, (b) transfer his or her expert skills to athletes to enhance their capability to achieve the goals, and to (c) provide the required resources and infrastructure to activate individual talent. Once the sporting event starts, the accountability for putting the game plan into action and for performance is transferred to the athletes. The focus of the athletes and coach then shifts to executing each task successfully during the game, in other words, to focus on specific inputs to achieve the best outcome. In this phase, the responsibility of the coach is to continuously monitor, support, encourage, and communicate, and to provide regular feedback and recognition. At half-time, both the coach and the athletes will review the scorecard and discuss ways to improve their performance. Athletes will also communicate what they need to perform better in the second half of the match. Rest is also important at the review period. The game then continues, and another review phase is done at the end of the game.

The same principles apply in the performance management process. In **Phase 1**, a higher-purpose vision, mission, and strategy must be established for the organization, and then it must be translated into individual goals. The employee and the leader should reach consensus on the goals, as this creates a partnership for performance. The role of the leader, in this phase, is to align the talent and life purpose of the employee to the requirements of a position and to the employee's goals, in support of the higher-purpose vision of the organization. The leader also needs to (a) ensure the employee is competent to achieve the goal, (b) provide the necessary resources to achieve the goal, and (c) create an effective work climate and culture to activate employee talent. Poor employee performance is often a reflection of poor leadership.

In **Phase 2**, responsibility is transferred to the employee, and both the employee and the leader focus on the daily inputs to achieve the desired outcomes. During this phase, the leader is responsible for serving and empowering the employee to achieve the set goals, and to provide the required support, encouragement, feedback, communication, and recognition. The leader must also regularly monitor progress on achievement of the goal.

In **Phase 3** of performance management, both the employee and the leader must review the scorecard, in other words, the outcomes. During a first review session, the leader and the employee review interim results together and discuss (a) what was done well, (b) what could be done better, and (c) what is needed to excel.

In **Phase 4** of the performance management process, a final review is done. During this phase, the employee and the leader review the final results.

A summary of the performance management process is presented in Figure 6.

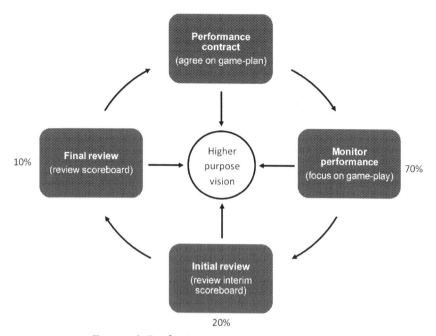

Figure 6. Performance management process

The Performance Stewardship Plan template, presented in Table 15, below, can be used in Phases 1, 3, and 4 of the performance management process, to set and review employee goals.

Table 15. Template for a Performance Stewardship Plan

Goal	Alpha	Current return	Omega	Future return	Omega
Goal 1	Agreement date	Desired mid-year outcome	Mid-year review date	Desired full-year outcome	Full-year review date
Goal 2	Agreement date	Desired mid-year outcome	Mid-year review date	Desired full-year outcome	Full-year review date
Goal 3	Agreement date	Desired mid-year outcome	Mid-year review date	Desired full-year outcome	Full-year review date
Goal 4	Agreement date	Desired mid-year outcome	Mid-year review date	Desired full-year outcome	Full-year review date
Goal 5	Agreement date	Desired mid-year outcome	Mid-year review date	Desired full-year outcome	Full-year review date

In the first column, employee goals can be listed, in line with the higher-purpose vision of the organization and in accordance with the life purpose of the employee. In the second column (*Alpha* column), the agreement or partnership date can be listed for each goal. In the fourth and sixth columns (*Omega* columns), the leader and the employee set review dates. In the *Current return* and *Future return* columns, the leader and the employee reach consensus on the desired outcomes to be achieved by the mid-year review and the full-year review. Specific recognition and rewards can also be listed in the *Current* and *Future return* columns.

Once a performance contract has been implemented, the leader and the employee should schedule regular check-in meetings to monitor progress and to determine how the leader could serve the employee to achieve the goal. Practical guidelines for these check-in sessions are discussed in the next chapter.

5.3 Improve products, processes, systems, policies, and procedures

The third objective of the steward-leadership function is to continuously improve the company's products, processes, systems, policies, and procedures. This is vital to an organization staying relevant in a constantly changing world. The first element that a leader should improve is the company's products and services. Many companies initially introduced a valuable product or service to the market, but as time progressed, the need of the customers and society changed, and the product and service of the company became irrelevant. Such companies failed to improve or to transform their products to create sustainable value for multiple stakeholders.

The primary factor in improving a company's products and services is to understand the changing needs of customers. Companies often only focus on selfish objectives when designing a new product, and do not consider the long-lasting impact it will have on people and society. Self-serving companies bargain on the greediness of mankind to buy its products, and they make use of immoral marketing techniques to sell their products. Companies should never design a new product or service with the intent to make money for the company and its shareholders to the detriment of other stakeholders, such as customers, employees, suppliers, society, and the environment. The true intent with a new or improved product should be to create sustainable value for people and society. A new product should thus serve the needs of people and society, not activate the greed of people.

The following questions can be helpful to understand when and how to improve a product or service:

- What is the true intent in developing or improving a product or service?
- Why is it necessary to improve or develop a new product or service?
- What value will the improved or newly developed product or service offer people and society?
- What will the long-term impact be of this product or service (on people and society)? Will the impact be constructive or destructive over the long term?
- What will drive customers to buy this product or service (greed or need)?
- What is the customer need this product or service satisfies?
- How can a product or service be improved to offer greater value for multiple stakeholders (customers, employees, organization, shareholders, suppliers, society, and the environment)?
- How can a product or service be improved to leave a long-lasting positive legacy for people, society, and the environment?

The second element to improve in an organization is its business processes and systems. Business processes and systems drive product delivery and customer service. It is thus important to frequently review business processes and systems and to make them more effective and efficient. This will also improve the effectiveness of the organization, which will reduce costs and increase revenue.

Leaders should always consider the impact on all stakeholders before implementing a business process or system. If a company implements a new system to the detriment of one stakeholder (by, for example, replacing employees with technology to make more profit), the improvement is in conflict with the core purpose of the business, namely to serve people and society (as discussed in Chapter 3). Improvements must always serve all stakeholders (customers, employees, shareholders, suppliers, society, and the environment).

The following questions could help to determine when and how to improve a business process and system:

- What is the reason for improvement?
- What will the long-term impact be on each stakeholder (customers, employees, shareholders, suppliers, society, and the environment) when we implement the new or improved business process or system?
- How can we improve a business process or system to create greater value for multiple stakeholders (customers, employees, shareholders, suppliers, society, and the environment)?

The third element to consider in continuously improving an organization is its policies and procedures. Policies and procedures should support the higher-purpose vision of the organization and serve multiple stakeholders, according to the core values of the company. It is therefore important to review the company's policies and procedures regularly to ensure these are aligned to the higher-purpose vision, mission, and strategy. Policies and procedures should also be updated to reflect any changes in legislation and to serve customers and employees better.

It is important to ensure the boundaries in policies and procedures are balanced. Policies and procedures that are too rigid may be barriers to excellent customer service and employee effectiveness, whereas policies and procedures that are too flexible could cause confusion or even chaos, which will also harm customer service and employee effectiveness. Policies and procedures should make it easier for employees to serve customers while maintaining certain boundaries, in line with the higher-purpose vision and values of the company.

The following questions could help to improve policies and procedures:

- What is the main purpose of the policy/procedure?
- Why is the policy/procedure necessary?
- How can the policy/procedure be improved to enhance customer service and employee effectiveness?

- How can the policy/procedure be improved to support the higher-purpose vision better?
- How can the policy be improved to build a better product or to render a better service to people and society?
- How can the policy be improved to help employees serve customers better?
- What impact will the new or updated policy/procedure have on customers, employees, shareholders, suppliers, society, and the environment?

Improvement analysis workshops can be an effective way to initiate improvements in products, processes, systems, policies, and procedures. An improvement workshop is a systematic workshop in which the employees and leaders closest to the product, process, system, policy, or procedure brainstorm ways to improve a product, process, system, policy, or procedure. Other stakeholders, such as customers and suppliers, could also be invited to these workshops; this will enrich conversations and provide additional insights into why and how a product, process, system, policy, or procedure could be improved.

The abovementioned questions can be used during an improvement workshop to initiate conversation. The Stop, Start, and Continue technique can thereafter be used to establish an action plan for improvement. The Stop, Start, and Continue technique includes three questions, namely: (1) What should we stop doing?, (2) What should we start doing?, and (3) What should we continue doing? Once all the questions have been answered and actions have been listed, the information gained through the workshop can be used to compile a formal strategy to improve the product, procedure, system, or policy.

5.4 Characteristics and competencies of the steward-leadership function

The first characteristic of the steward-leadership function is accountability. Accountability can be defined as being responsible and holding others accountable by continuously monitoring one's own performance and that of others. Accountability also includes setting clear expectations, in accordance with the higher-purpose vision of the organization and the capability and life purpose of the individual.

The competency of stewardship is also required to apply the steward-leadership objectives. This competency can be defined as the ability to look after the common interests of multiple stakeholders (customers, employees, the organization, suppliers, shareholders, society, and the environment), and to leave a positive legacy in the world, with a life perspective of being a caretaker-in-life, rather than an owner-in-life. It is important to equip leaders with the knowledge, skills, and ability to be good stewards to create long-lasting value for multiple stakeholders with a loving heart.

CHAPTER 6
THE FARMER-LEADERSHIP FUNCTION

The fourth function of a servant-leader is to align, care for, and grow employees. This function falls within the operational servant-leadership domain and is part of the *hands* dimension of servant leadership. The analogy of a farmer is used to describe this function. The objectives, characteristics, and competencies of the farmer-leadership function are discussed in this chapter, and practical guidelines are provided to implement this function effectively in the workplace.

A farmer is someone who knows plants or livestock well and has expertise regarding the choice of seed or animal to nurture. The main purpose of a farmer is to harvest a plant for a higher purpose. A farmer plants the right seed in the ground and thereafter cares for it by providing the correct amount of water, sunlight, fertilizer, pruning, and temperature to grow the plant. The farmer then harvests the product for a greater good — to feed thousands of people.

A farmer knows that certain seeds grow only in specific environments. For instance, a farmer knows that vines will struggle to grow in the desert, but will flourish in areas with regular sun and rain, where there is little frost and hail. A farmer also knows that too much sun and water will damage a vineyard, and that an entire harvest could be lost in this way. A farmer therefore has the knowledge of (a) different types of seeds, (b) which seeds are more likely to grow in certain environmental and weather conditions, (c) what a seed needs to grow and flourish, and (d) how to grow and harvest a seed for a higher purpose. A farmer puts in a lot of effort to care for the seed by supplying everything it needs to grow and by protecting the seed from anything that could damage it. The main purpose of a farmer is thus to (a) select the right seed, (b) provide the right conditions for the seed to grow, (c) help the seed grow, and then to (d) harvest the fruit of the seed for a higher purpose.

The same principles apply to leadership. A leader needs to select the right employees for the organization. Once the employees have been selected (planted), the leader must care for the employees by creating the right work climate, culture, and conditions, and serve their individual needs, to activate the talent and potential of these employees. A leader should also grow employees continuously and be able to harvest individual talent and potential, with the aim of achieving the higher-purpose vision of the organization. A leader must therefore know (a) which types of individuals will fit the organization and its climate and culture the best, (b) what the employees need in order to flourish, and (c) how to grow and harvest individual talent for a greater good. A leader should continuously ask him- or herself the following question: Who needs me? These functions of the farmer-leadership function are summarized in Table 16, and are discussed in more detail below.

Table 16. The objectives, characteristics, and competencies of the farmer-leadership function (Coetzer et al. 2017)

Function	Align, care for, and grow employees
Leadership question	Who needs me?
Objectives	• Align employees • Care for employees • Grow employees
Characteristics	• Listening • Compassion
Competency	• Building relationships • Empowerment

6.1 Align employees

Aligning employees means to align the purpose, talent, knowledge, skills, values, and personality of an individual to the requirements of a position and to the higher-purpose vision of the organization. Aligning employees is crucial in recruitment and selection processes, as it would be very difficult to grow and activate individual talent if it is misaligned with the organization and its vision. To use the analogy of the farmer, when the farmer plants a vine in the desert, it would be near impossible to grow and activate the fruit of the vine. However, if the alignment between a seed and the environment is done properly, activating and growing the seed become easy, almost automatic.

The same is true when aligning employees. When misalignment occurs during recruitment and selection, it is very difficult to grow and motivate an individual to perform consistently and to access that person's talents in order to achieve the higher-purpose vision of the organization. However, if the employee's life purpose, talents, knowledge, skills, value, and personality are accurately aligned to the requirements of the position and to the higher-purpose vision of the organization, it is much easier to achieve. Employees will then experience intrinsic motivation and will be driven by a higher cause to perform. Employee alignment can be done in two ways, namely person–job fit and person–organization fit.

6.1.1   Person–job fit

Person–job fit refers to the alignment between a person's life purpose, knowledge, skills, talent, and personality, and the requirements of a position as defined in the Job Profile, which describes the key responsibilities, educational and experience requirements, as well as the required attributes to be successful in the position. This is called *positional alignment*.

It is important to first establish a higher-purpose vision for the company (as discussed in Chapter 3) and then to profile each position in the company before positional or organizational alignment can be done during recruitment and selection processes.

A Job Profile can be used to determine person–job fit. A Job Profile is a summary of the key responsibilities of a position and the knowledge, skills, and attributes required to be successful in the position. During a person–job fit analysis, a specific Job Profile can be used to compare a person's life purpose, knowledge, skills, and attributes with the requirements of the position as listed in the Job Profile. A person–job fit analysis is done as follows:

- The life purpose of a person is compared with the key responsibilities of the position.
- The qualifications of the person are compared with the educational requirements of the position.
- The experience and abilities of the person are compared with the skills required for the position.
- The personality of the person is compared with the attributes required for the position.

Three tools can be used to conduct a person–job fit analysis, namely a (1) CV Screening Scorecard, (2) Competency-based Interview Guide, and a (3) Psychometric Assessment Scorecard. A CV Screening Scorecard lists the main qualification and experience required for a position and provides a scorecard with which to evaluate whether a person meets these requirements. It excludes the name, gender, and race of applicants, and only evaluates their qualification and experience. The Scorecard is then used to score each CV, and applicants are ranked. The top two to four candidates can thereafter be invited for an interview. An example of a CV Screening Scorecard is provided in Appendix A.

A second tool that can be used in the person–job fit process is a Competency-based Interview Guide. This Guide contains a list of questions regarding the competencies relevant to a specific position, and includes a rating scale for each question. Competency-based questions evaluate the competency level of a person in relation to the competencies listed in the Job Profile. The top five competencies of a position are normally used to develop this Guide. Two to three questions to assess each competency are then formulated and listed in the Interview Guide.

An interview panel could use the Competency-based Interview Guide to evaluate a person's competence during a job interview and to score an individual accordingly. Afterwards, the interview panel could consolidate and discuss the scores of each application and reach consensus on the final scores for each candidate. These final scores are then used to select the top two candidates. An example of a Competency-based Interview Guide is provided in Appendix A.

The Interview Guide could also include questions to evaluate the life purpose of an individual in comparison with the purpose of the position. The key responsibilities listed in a Job Profile can also be compared with the life purpose of an individual. A score can then be allocated by the interview panel, to determine which candidate shows the best fit.

The third tool that can be used in the person–job fit process is a Psychometric Assessment Scorecard. This lists (a) the ability, behavioral, and other attributes required to be successful in a position, (b) a benchmark for each factor relevant to a specific position, and (c) scores for assessment results above or below the benchmark. Industrial and organizational psychologists could use Psychometric Assessment Scorecards to compare the assessment results of an individual with the required ability, behavioral, and other attributes of a position, to calculate a final assessment score for an individual. The top two candidates identified by the interview panel are normally invited to complete psychometric assessments. Psychologists can then use the Psychometric Assessment Scorecard to determine the best person–job fit for the position. An example of a Psychometric Assessment Scorecard is provided in Appendix A.

It is important to note that psychometric assessments should not be used in isolation to make final decisions. A selection panel should rather use all the information retrieved from the CV Screening Scorecard, Competency-based Interview Guide, and the Psychometric Assessment Scorecard, as well as any other relevant source (such as reference letters, background checks, simulations, etc.) to make a final decision on which candidate is the best fit for the position.

6.1.2   Person–organization fit

The second type of alignment is person–organization fit, which refers to an alignment of a person's values, personality, and life purpose with the values, culture, and higher purpose of the organization. When person–organization fit is done well, the employee will experience high levels of intrinsic motivation (self-motivation), energy, and life satisfaction. With higher levels of motivation, energy, and life satisfaction, employees will perform better. Employees will thus provide better customer service, produce better products and services, and achieve work goals sooner. This will enhance organizational performance and increase the probability of the organization achieving the higher-purpose vision.

The higher-purpose vision statement, the Organizational Values Framework, and the creed of a company can be used to determine person–organization fit. The higher-purpose vision statement is a description of (a) the higher purpose of the organization, (b) how the organization creates value for multiple stakeholders (customers, employees, suppliers, shareholders, society, and the environment), and (c) what type of legacy the organization wants to leave in the world. The Organizational Values Framework describes the values of the organization, together with the behavioral indicators for each value, in other words, how each value is measured in the organization. An organizational creed summarizes the main principles and practices of the organization and is a consolidation of a company's higher-purpose vision and the values required to achieve that vision. It therefore describes why the organization exists, what the organization aims to achieve, and how employees should behave in the organization.

A leader can determine person–organization fit by:

- Comparing the life purpose of an individual with the higher-purpose vision statement of the organization;
- Comparing the values of a person with the Organizational Values Framework; and
- Comparing the behavioral traits of a person with the organizational creed of the company.

Psychometric assessments can be used to compare a person's values and behavioral traits with the values of the organization and the behaviors listed in the organizational creed. The individual's view of his or her purpose can be established in a job interview and then compared with the higher-purpose vision of the organization. In this way, the life purpose, values, and behavioral attributes of an individual are used to determine person–organization fit. An example of an Organizational Values Framework and an organizational creed are provided in Appendix A.

6.2 Care for employees

Once a leader has selected the right employees for the organization, he or she must care for them by serving their needs and by creating a conducive work environment.

Caring for employees means to create a conducive work climate and culture in the organization, in which employees can flourish. Such an organizational climate and culture will activate individual talent and potential, and will enhance employees' engagement in their work. Employees will then experience high levels of energy and motivation and will be committed to achieving the higher-purpose vision of the organization. Leaders are responsible for creating such an organizational climate and culture within a company.

An organizational culture refers to the values, principles, and practices in the company, whereas an organizational climate refers to the work environment and conditions in the organization. Leaders are responsible for creating an organizational climate and culture in which employees can grow quickly, perform optimally, and experience job satisfaction. Before a leader can create such a climate and culture, he or she needs to understand what employees need in order to flourish. A leader must know exactly what employees need in order to be engaged in their work and to grow as individuals, in the same way a farmer must know what a seed needs to grow and flourish.

When a new seed is planted in the ground, a farmer needs to serve the needs of the seed to ensure it grows into a plant, to ultimately harvest its fruit for a greater good. The general needs of a seed are: the right temperature, continuous water, adequate fertilizer, healthy sunlight, regular pruning, sufficient time, and enough room to grow. The same applies to leading people. Employees need the correct workload (temperature), continuous learning and development (water), adequate physical resources (fertilizer), healthy relationships with colleagues and the leader (sunlight), regular performance feedback and guidance (pruning), sufficient time to grow in a career (time), and enough autonomy (room) to flourish. The Job Demands–Resources Model explains this well.

According to the Job Demands–Resources Model, employees will become engaged in their work when they experience a balance between job demands and job resources (Bakker & Demerouti 2007). Job demands are the demands of the job that drain energy, such as workload, emotional load, and mental load (De Braine & Roodt 2011). The workload is the physical aspects of a job, whereas the emotional load is the emotional strain related to the job, such as dealing with difficult customers, working with a demanding manager or colleague, or working in difficult circumstances. Mental load refers to cognitive weariness. Many of us today work mentally, not physically. The human brain can also become overloaded and tired. Symptoms of cognitive weariness include forgetfulness and finding it difficult to focus.

Job resources, on the other hand, are those aspects of the job that buffer the negative effects of high job demands, such as organizational resources, developmental resources, social resources, and positional resources (Schaufeli 2015).

6.2.1 *Organizational resources*

Organizational resources include (a) adequate and regular communication, (b) remuneration, and (c) physical resources. Employees will feel a sense of belonging when they are involved in decision-making processes and leaders regularly communicate to them what is happening in the organization, as well as what they should focus on to achieve the organization's goals. Employees also need adequate and regular remuneration and recognition for their work. Regular recognition boosts self-confidence and extrinsic motivation, which will, in turn, increase work performance. Adequate remuneration ensures a quality life for employees and their families. Remuneration should never be the main reason for working, but rather a source an employee can use to serve others. Employees also need physical resources to do their work, such as a computer, desk, telephone, etc.

6.2.2 *Developmental resources*

The second type of job resources an employee needs is developmental resources. These resources include (a) performance feedback, (b) learning and development opportunities, (c) self-perceived competence, and (d) a career path. Employees need performance feedback in the same way a tree needs pruning to grow in the right direction. Regular performance feedback will ensure employees know what is expected of them, what they did well, and how they could excel. Performance review sessions also provide employees with an opportunity to indicate what they need in order to perform. Performance feedback thus requires two-way communication and a partnership to achieve goals in line with the higher-purpose vision of the organization.

Learning and development opportunities refer to any activity that enhances individual knowledge, skill, and competence. Learning and development opportunities include foundational learning activities (such as formal education programs, short courses, and workshops), experiential learning activities (such as simulations, on-the-job training, job rotation, and workplace assignments), and transformational learning activities (such as coaching and mentoring).

Self-perceived competence refers to how competent an employee feels. It is important for leaders to always try and build the self-confidence of employees, as work performance generally increases when employees' self-confidence increases. When employees doubt themselves, they will hesitate to take on new challenges, and their mental view of what they are capable of will limit their performance.

Employees also need a career path in the organization — a future position to work towards. It is, however, important that a career path be guided by the employee, not the employer. The career path should be aligned to the individual's life purpose, talents, interests, and potential. Sometimes, it is necessary to prepare an employee for a career outside of the organization if the organization cannot offer such a career internally. This is one of the benefits of working for a serving organization.

6.2.3   Social resources

The third type of job resources employees need is social resources. These resources include healthy relationships with supervisors and colleagues and effective leadership practices in the organization. Employees need healthy relationships at work to be engaged in their work. Many employees do not leave organizations, they leave managers and colleagues. Employees sometimes spend more time with the people at work than they do with their spouse and children. A typical worker will spend approximately eight hours at work, two hours in traffic, two hours on extramural activities, eight hours sleeping, and maybe four hours with their spouse and children. People also often work on weekends. With technology to work digitally, many people never stop working, even when they are at home with their family. It is therefore important to ensure that employees experience healthy work relationships as these relationships influence them the most.

Unhealthy work relationships might also have a spillover effect. For example, when an employee experiences conflict with a manager at work, he or she might bring negative emotions home, which will then negatively influence the relationship with his or her spouse or children. Unhealthy relationships at home might also have a negative spillover effect on work. This is a negative cycle that could hinder work performance. However, if employees experience healthy relationships at work, they will return home in a healthy emotional state, which will positively influence their relationships with their spouse and children. When healthy relationships are experienced at home, an employee will return to work refreshed and energized. It is therefore important to cultivate healthy work relationships, and to stop any emotional spillover effect.

Leadership practices in an organization are also crucial to engage employees. For instance, if employees experience autocratic or ineffective leadership practices, their performance will be driven by either fear or greed. However, when effective leadership practices and behavior exist in an organization, employees will be self-motivated, energized, and will want to excel at their work. It is thus important to establish effective leadership practices in the organization.

6.2.4   *Positional resources*

The fourth type of job resource is positional resources. These resources include adequate person–job fit, role clarity, and job information. When an adequate person–job fit is ensured in the recruitment and selection process, it will be easier for employees to activate and deploy their knowledge, skills, and talents in line with the requirements of the position. With improper person–job fit, employees struggle to deploy their true self in a position.

Employees also need job clarity and job information to be successful in a position. Job clarity and information include information and knowledge on (a) how the position supports the higher-purpose vision of the company, (b) what is expected of the employee in the position, (c) clear employee goals, and (d) the employee knowing how to succeed in a position. Without this knowledge and understanding, it would be very difficult for employees to excel in their jobs.

Research indicates that meaningful job demands coupled with adequate job resources increase the level of work engagement of employees (Bakker & Demerouti 2007). Work engagement is an individual state in which the employee experiences high vigor (energy), dedication (motivation), and absorption (focus) while working (Schaufeli, Bakker, & Salanova 2006). Several individual and organizational benefits are associated with high work engagement levels. For example, employees who experience high levels of work engagement are more committed to the organization and are more productive, perform better, and are less inclined to leave the organization. Such employees also render a better customer service. High work engagement is furthermore associated with lower absenteeism, presenteeism, and fewer industrial relations issues and safety incidents in the workplace.

Conversely, research also indicates that high job demands with inadequate job resources cause employee burnout (Bakker & Demerouti 2007). Burnout is a negative human state characterized by exhaustion (low energy), depersonalization or detachment from work (low motivation), and low personal accomplishment (due to a lack of focus) (Schaufeli 2003). Burnout, in turn, causes physical or psychological ill health. When employees experience physical or psychological ill health, their performance and productivity decrease. In this case, employees will be more inclined to leave the organization and will render poor customer service. Physical or psychological ill health will, furthermore, cause more absenteeism, presenteeism, and an increase in industrial relations issues and safety incidents in the workplace.

The balance or imbalance between job demands and job resources will thus either initiate a motivational process or a health impairment process (Schaufeli & Bakker 2004). A motivational process will be activated when employees experience meaningful job demands with adequate job resources, which will increase their levels of work engagement and result in positive individual and organizational outcomes. A health impairment process, in contrast, will be activated when employees experience high job demands in the absence of the required job resources, which will cause employee burnout and result in negative individual and organizational outcomes. These two processes are summarized in the Job Demands–Resources Model (Bakker & Demerouti 2007). The Job Demands–Resources Model (also known as the Work-wellness Model) is therefore a prediction model that predicts which employee- and organizational inputs will lead to specific employee or organizational outputs (Rothmann 2008). If leaders want high levels of productivity, performance, and customer service and low employee turnover, absenteeism, labor action, and safety accidents, they need to provide meaningful job demands and adequate job resources to employees. A summary of the Job Demands–Resources Model is presented in Figure 7.

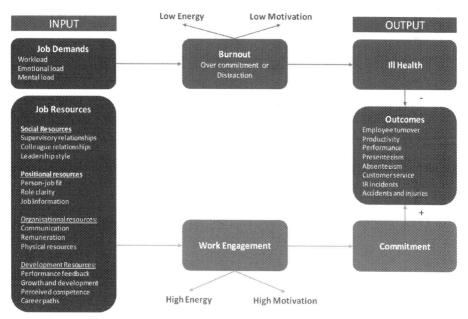

Figure 7. Summary of the Job Demands–
Resources Model (Rothmann 2008)

Leaders must understand how employees experience the current job demands and job resources in an organization before they can effectively manage these. It is thus important to regularly measure how employees experience the current work climate and the organizational climate. The experience of job demands and job resources will also differ from one employee to another and from one department to the next. It is therefore important to diagnose the experience of job demands and job resources per individual, per department, and for the whole organization. National and international benchmarks could also be helpful to understand how an organization performs against national, international, or industry benchmarks.

One way to measure the organizational climate of an organization is to use the Organizational Human Factor Benchmark (OHFB) instrument of Afriforte (Pty) Ltd. This instrument measures the experience of job demands and job resources in an organization, as well as the levels of work engagement, burnout, ill health, and organizational commitment (organizational citizenship behavior). It also identifies drivers and risks related to human capital. More information on the instrument can be retrieved from Afriforte's website (www.afriforte.co.za). This is only one of many instruments available to measure organizational climate, but certainly one of the best.

An alternative way to understand how employees experience job demands and resources in the company is to simply ask them in a personal meeting. The following questions might be helpful to diagnose an employee's experience of job demands and job resources, and to understand ways to improve these:

- How do you experience your current workload, mental load, and emotional load?
- What can we do to reduce your workload, mental load, and emotional load?
- How do you experience the social resources (colleague relationships, supervisor relationships, and leadership practice) of the work unit?
- What can we do to improve the colleague relationships, supervisory relationships, and leadership practices in our work unit?
- How do you experience the positional resources (person–job fit, job clarity, and job information) in the work unit?
- How can we enhance your levels of person–job fit?
- What type of job information do you need more of?
- How can we make your job expectations clearer?

- How do you experience the organizational resources (communication, remuneration, and physical resources) in the work unit?
- What type of organizational information would you like more of?
- What type of recognition would you prefer?
- Which physical resources do you need?
- How do you experience the developmental resources (performance feedback, growth and development opportunities, self-perceived competence, and career paths)?
- How regularly would you like to receive performance feedback?
- In which areas would you like to grow personally?
- What type of learning activities would you enjoy?
- How confident do you feel to execute your job tasks successfully?
- What can we do to enhance your self-perceived confidence?
- What would be the ideal job for you in the future?
- How can the organization assist to create the ideal job for you?

Once leaders have diagnosed the current organizational climate in terms of demands and resources, they must identify any organizational development areas from the results, and design and implement appropriate interventions to address those areas. Leaders should also re-evaluate the organizational climate after an intervention has been implemented, to determine if the intervention was successful. It is important to diagnose the climate of the organization regularly, as it could change over time. The process of diagnosis, intervention, and re-evaluation should be done at least annually.

In summary, leaders should care for employees by creating a conducive work climate and conditions by providing the necessary job resources to employees and managing their job demands, and also by monitoring and improving their levels of work engagement and organizational commitment. Employees will then respond with higher productivity and performance with which to achieve the higher-purpose vision of the organization.

6.3 Grow employees

After a farmer has planted the right seed and created suitable conditions for growth, the farmer must grow the seed by serving its needs and then harvest the fruit of the seed for a greater good. The third objective of the farmer-leadership function is thus to grow employees. Growing employees refers to the process of empowering employees in line with their life purpose to execute the higher-purpose vision of the organization by means of continuous training and development. During this development process, employee talent is activated and employee potential is unlocked for a greater good. When employees continuously grow and develop, their competence levels increase, which will enhance their ability to perform.

The purpose of growth is, firstly, to empower employees and, secondly, to transfer accountability to them. Employees must first be competent to do a task before accountability for executing that task can be transferred to them. Leaders often delegate tasks to individuals without taking the time to empower them, and then complain when employees do not complete the task in time or according to the set standards. Empowering employees means equipping individuals with the knowledge, skills, and resources to do a job well, and then transferring accountability to the employee. After empowering the employee, the leader should continue to support and grow the employee, to ensure high levels of job performance are maintained.

There are three basic reasons why employees perform poorly in a job or task, namely a (1) lack of energy, (2) lack of competence, or (3) lack of motivation. An employee can be highly competent and motivated to complete a task, but if he or she experiences low levels of energy, it would be very difficult for the individual to apply his or her competence and motivation. Another scenario is when an employee has the energy and motivation to complete a task, but does not know how to do it. In other words, the employee lacks competence. In this scenario, the employee will also perform poorly. A third scenario is when an employee has the energy and competence to complete a task, but lacks motivation. In this case, the employee will also perform poorly, because he or she is not motivated to apply his or her energy and competence. All three factors (energy, competence, and motivation) are thus required to sustain high performance.

The three dimensions of energy, competence, and motivation also work in synergy. For example, energy is required to complete learning activities to become competent. When a person has become competent, he or she will experience positive emotions when applying the new skill and successfully completing a task. Motivational levels therefore increase with an increase in competence. When an individual is highly motivated to complete a task, his or her energy level will increase. A positive cycle thus starts with high energy and flows as follows: high energy increases competence, high competence increases motivation, and high motivation increases energy. The opposite is also true. When people lack energy, they will not be able to acquire a new skill effectively, and will then become discouraged or unmotivated because they cannot master the new skill or complete a task successfully. This will drain their energy. In this case, a negative cycle is initiated by the lack of energy. The synergetic cycle of the three dimensions of energy, competence, and motivation is presented in Figure 8.

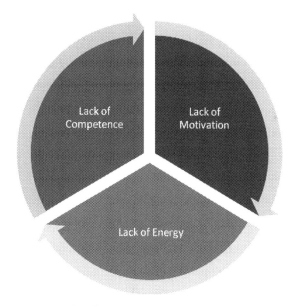

Figure 8. Cycle of energy, competence, and motivation

Levels of energy, competence, and motivation are always dependent on the specific task or goal. For example, an employee might be competent, motivated, and energized to do a sales pitch, but might be unmotivated to compile a sales report. It is thus important to diagnose an employee's level of energy, competence, and motivation per task or per goal. Once a leader has diagnosed an employee's level of energy, competence, and motivation per task or goal, he or she must provide the required recovery (when energy is low), development (when competence is low), and support (when motivation is low).

One way to empower employees is to apply the Recover, Develop, and Support Model. This model is a combination of the Situational Leadership Model (Blanchard, Zigarmi, Zigarmi, & Halsey 2013), the Job Demands–Resources Model (Bakker & Demerouti 2007), and the Tell, Ask, Problem, and Solution (TAPS) Model (Gunter 2013). The Situational Leadership Model (Blanchard et al. 2013) suggests that a leader should first diagnose an employee's level of competence and motivation, and thereafter apply one of four leadership approaches to address the employee's needs. The Job Demands–Resources Model (Bakker & Demerouti 2007) suggests that a leader should diagnose the work engagement (energy and motivation) of an employee, and thereafter manage the job demands and job resources of employees, to enhance the employee's energy and motivation. The TAPS Model differentiates between four leader approaches, namely coaching, counselling, teaching, and consulting (Gunter 2013). In the coaching approach, the leader asks questions to identify a solution, whereas, in the counselling approach, the leader asks questions to identify the problem. In the teaching approach, the leader tells the employee what the solution is, whereas, in the consulting approach, the leader tells the employee what the problem is.

The Recover, Develop, and Support (RDS) Model recommends three steps to empower employees: (1) review the goal, (2) diagnose the employee's level of energy, competence, and motivation, and (3) apply the correct leader approach to address the needs of the employee.

6.3.1   *Review the goal*

It is important to review the goal before starting diagnosis, because a person's levels of energy, motivation, and energy will differ per task or goal. The first step is therefore for the leader and the employee to review the goal first and to ensure the goal is specific, measurable, attainable, relevant, and time-based (SMART). The goal should also be in line with the higher-purpose vision of the organization and the life purpose of the individual.

6.3.2   Diagnose levels of energy, competence, and motivation

Once the goal has been reviewed, a leader should diagnose the employee's levels of energy, competence, and motivation in relation to the goal. In this step, a leader must create a safe environment for the employee to speak freely, and should ask the employee how energized, competent, and motivated he or she feels to achieve the goal. It is also important to do this diagnosis together with the employee, not in isolation.

An application tool is provided in Appendix A to diagnose the energy, competence, and motivation levels of the employee, named the Leader–Employee Diagnostic Form. The first step in applying this tool is to review the goal, in other words, to establish the employee's goal and to ensure it is 'SMART'. Once the goal has been reviewed, the leader and employee can move on to diagnosing the energy, competence, and motivation levels of the employee in relation to the goal. This is done by allocating a score between 1 and 10 to each dimension on the form and by plotting the scores on the graph provided. The score for each dimension should be plotted on all three lines of the dimension. For example, if the employee's score for *Energy* is 2, then a mark should be made at the number 2 level on all three green lines. If the employee's score for *Competence* is, e.g., 5, then a mark should be made at the number 5 level on all three orange lines. The same should be done on the blue lines for *Motivation*. Afterwards, the lines can be connected to reveal which areas are the lowest. Once diagnosed, the employee can identify on the form what type of recovery, development, or support he or she needs to achieve the goal. The leader can also select an appropriate leader approach on the form.

6.3.3   Apply the correct leader approach

After diagnosis, a leader must apply the correct leadership approach to either help recover the employee's energy levels, develop his or her competence, or support the employee to regain motivation. The job demands and job resources listed in the Job Demands–Resources Model could be useful to enhance energy, competence, and motivation. For example, when the energy level of an employee is low, the employee needs recovery. Recovery can then be initiated by decreasing the job demands of the employee. Workload, for instance, can be reduced by prioritizing tasks and by completing the most important and urgent tasks first. Mental load can be decreased by helping the employee to focus on completing one task at a time. Emotional load can be lessened by enabling the employee to cope with difficult people or circumstances. Energy levels can also be recovered by providing the employee with more rest in the form of leave or an enhanced work–life balance.

When the competence level of an employee is low, a leader must provide more developmental job resources, such as constructive performance feedback or training and development opportunities. A leader could also provide coaching and mentoring to enhance the employee's self-perceived competence. Training, coaching, and mentoring might also be useful to prepare an employee for the next position in his or her career path.

When the motivation level of an employee is low, a leader must provide more social, positional, and organizational resources. These job resources include (a) improving supervisor and colleague relationships, (b) applying more effective leadership practices, (c) ensuring a good person–job fit, (d) providing more job clarity and information and explaining why a goal is important, (e) sharing important company information with the employee, (f) increasing remuneration or recognition, and (g) providing more physical resources. The key, however, is to ask the employee what he or she needs and what would enhance his or her motivation to achieve the goal.

A summary of the required job resources per dimension is provide in Figure 9.

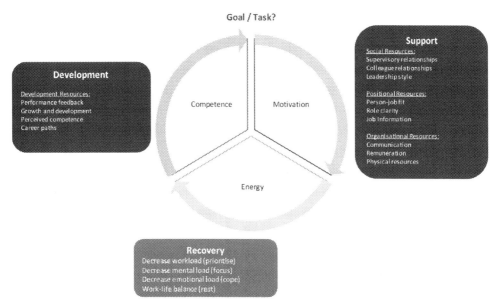

Figure 9. Required job resources to remedy low
levels of energy, competence, or motivation

Four different leader approaches can be applied to help the employee recover (when energy is low), to develop (when competence is low), and to support (when motivation is low), namely (1) coaching, (2) counselling, (3) consulting, and (4) training. The leader approach is selected according to the lowest value dimension identified during diagnosis. For example, if an employee indicated a score of 3 for energy, 6 for competence, and a score of 9 for motivation during the diagnosis, the lowest value dimension is energy. A specific leader approach should then be selected to enhance energy levels. The four different leader approaches are discussed in more detail below.

6.3.3.1 Coaching approach

The coaching approach is appropriate when an employee's level of motivation is the lowest score. In this case, the employee is competent (knows how to complete the task) and energized (able to complete the task), but lacks motivation (does not want to complete the task). The leader should then ask the employee questions related to finding a solution. It would be counterproductive to tell the employee how to recover his or her energy or how to do the job or gain more energy, as the employee is already competent and has a high level of energy. It is thus important that the leader ask the employee to initiate a solution and to frame the questions in terms of social, positional, and organizational resources required.

6.3.3.2 Counselling approach

The counselling approach is appropriate when the employee's energy level is the lowest score and his or her level of motivation is the second-lowest score. In this scenario, the employee is competent (knows how to complete the task) and experiences low to average motivation (sometimes wants to complete the task), but lacks energy (is not able to complete the task). A leader should then ask questions to understand the foundational cause of the problem and focus on decreasing the job demands of the employee, such as workload, mental load, and emotional load.

6.3.3.3 Consulting approach

The consulting approach is appropriate when the employee's level of energy is the lowest score and level of competence is the second-lowest score. In this scenario, the employee has a high level of motivation (wants to complete the task) and a low to average level of competence (could complete the task with guidance), but lacks energy (is not able to complete the task). In this case, the leader must guide the employee to understand the problem and focus on decreasing the job demands of the employee. Guidance is required in this scenario, as the employee is not yet competent to understand the problem and to implement solutions.

6.3.3.4 Training approach

The training approach is required when the employee's competence level was identified as the lowest in the diagnosis. In this case, the employee experiences high motivation (wants to complete the task) and high energy (is able to complete the task), but lacks the competence (does not know how to complete the task). The leader should then guide or tell the employee what the solution is, because the employee does not yet know how to complete the task. Development job resources might be useful to enhance competence in this scenario, such as constructive performance feedback, training and development opportunities, mentoring and coaching to enhance self-perceived competence, and preparing an employee for a next position in his or her career path.

In this case, it would frustrate and demotivate the employee if the leader, for example, asks the employee what the solution is (coaching approach), because the employee does not know the answer. It is therefore important to diagnose the levels of energy, competence, and motivation of an employee correctly (with the employee), and then to apply the appropriate leader approach to meet the needs of the employee.

A graphical display of the four approaches is provided in Figure 10.

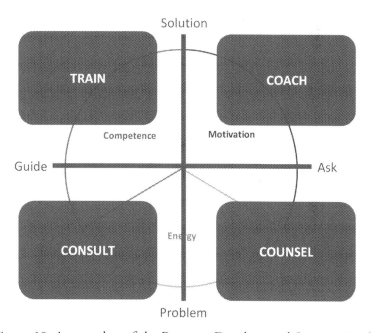

Figure 10. Approaches of the Recover, Develop, and Support Model

The horizontal axis represents the *Communication* continuum, from *Guiding* to *Asking*. The communication continuum therefore indicates whether a leader should ask questions or tell the person what to do. The vertical axis represents the *Focus* continuum, from *Solution-focused* to *Problem-focused*. The *Focus* continuum indicates to the leader when to focus on the root cause of a problem and when to focus on generating a solution.

A guide to applying each leader approach is provided in Appendix A. A leader could use these guides, after diagnosing the levels of energy, competence, and motivation of the employee, as a framework in a one-on-one meeting with the employee. It is important to choose the appropriate approach before engaging with the employee, as the wrong approach will have a negative impact on the employee. A summary of the Recover, Develop, and Support Model is provided in Figure 11.

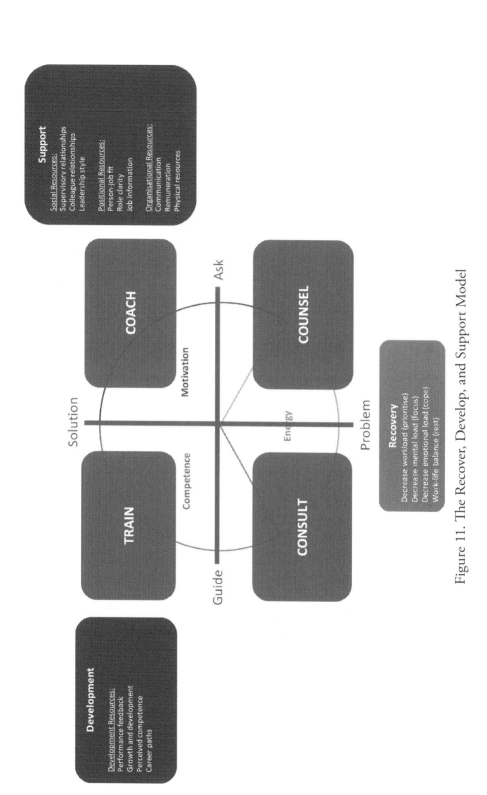

Figure 11. The Recover, Develop, and Support Model

6.4 The characteristics and competencies of the farmer-leadership function

The characteristics associated with the farmer-leadership function are: listening and compassion. Listening means to (a) listen actively and respectfully to others, (b) ask questions to clarify a message or create knowledge, (c) provide time for reflection and silence, and to (d) be conscious of what is unsaid. Compassion refers to (a) being empathetic, caring, and kind, (b) forgiving others for past mistakes, (c) accepting and appreciating others for who they are, (d) treating others with unconditional love, (e) valuing and serving others, (f) helping people recover from hardship and difficulties, and (g) enhancing the professional wellbeing of others. Listening will help leaders to identify and understand the needs of employees. Compassion will drive a leader to serve the needs of employees and to activate their talent and potential to achieve the higher-purpose vision of the company and their own life purpose.

The competencies associated with the farmer-leadership function are: building relationships and empowerment. Building relationships refers to the ability to (a) build trustful relationships with individuals, customers, and the community, (b) create a work environment characterized by care, support, encouragement, and acknowledgement, (c) communicate effectively by spending quality time with employees, (d) understand the needs, aspirations, potential, and mental model of others, (e) work in collaboration with others, and to (f) share values. The competency of empowerment is defined as the ability to (a) develop others to prosper personally, professionally, and spiritually, (b) transform and influence direct reports, (c) transfer responsibility and authority to direct reports, (d) provide clear directions and boundaries, (e) align and activate individual talent, (f) share information, (g) encourage independent problem-solving, (h) provide coaching, mentoring, and support according to the needs of direct reports, (i) create an effective work environment, (j) build self-confidence, wellbeing, and proactive behavior, and to (k) help employees mature emotionally, intellectually, and ethically. Leaders will use the competency of building relationships to build trustful relationships with employees and then use the competency of empowerment to empower employees to obtain the higher-purpose vision of the company as well as the life purpose of employees.

A servant-leader therefore needs the characteristics of listening and compassion and the competencies of building relationships and empowerment to apply the three objectives of the farmer-leadership function, namely to align, care for, and grow employees.

PART 4

IMPLEMENTING SERVANT LEADERSHIP

Part 1 of this book discussed the *heart* dimension of a servant-leader, which refers to the intent and values of a servant-leader (*why* a servant-leader leads others). Part 2 discussed the *head* dimension of a servant-leader, which refers to strategic servant leadership (*what* a servant-leader wants to achieve). Part 3 explained the *hands* dimension of a servant-leader, which refers to operational servant leadership (*how* a servant-leader leads others).

In Part 4 of this book, several frameworks and practical guidelines are provided to apply the four functions of servant leadership (the soldier-, athlete-, steward-, and farmer-leadership functions) systematically in an organization. Chapter 7 provides practical frameworks to train and cultivate servant-leaders in an organization. Chapter 8 summarizes the four functions of servant leadership in one model and provides an implementation procedure to apply servant leadership systematically in an organization.

CHAPTER 7
FRAMEWORKS TO DEVELOP SERVANT-LEADERS

In the previous chapters, the four functions of a servant-leader were comprehensively discussed. Application tools for the functions were also provided, which could be used in any context. In this chapter, two frameworks are provided to develop servant-leaders in an organization. Each framework is accompanied by a systematic process for cultivating and training servant-leaders in an organization.

The first framework is the Talent Wheel of Servant Leadership, which is an informal approach to transforming an employee into a servant-leader. The process is informal because it is a one-on-one approach, between the leader and the employee. The second framework, the Framework for Effective Servant-leadership Development, entails a formal process of systematic implementation of a servant-leadership development program in an organization.

7.1 Talent Wheel of Servant Leadership

The general aim of the Talent Wheel of Servant Leadership is to transform employees into servant-leaders, which is one of the ultimate goals of being a servant-leader (Greenleaf 1998). Servant-leaders must continuously strive to transform employees into servant-leaders to replace the leaders when their leadership period ends. The organization will then have a good bench-strength of leaders available to occupy future leadership positions as the organization grows.

The Talent Wheel of Servant Leadership summarizes the four functions of a servant-leader into a wheel framework and proposes four developmental phases to transform an employee into a servant-leader, namely the (1) athlete-transformation phase, (2) farmer-transformation phase, (3) steward-transformation phase, and the (4) soldier-transformation phase (Coetzer 2018b). A graphical display of the Talent Wheel of Servant Leadership is presented in Figure 12.

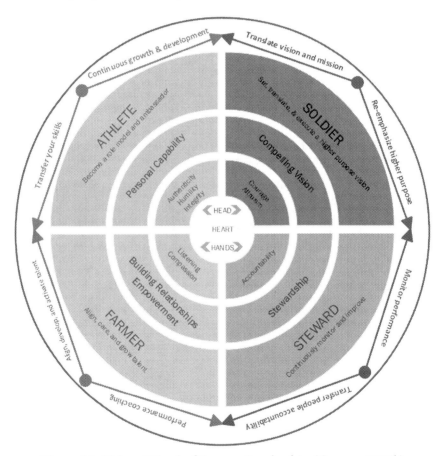

Figure 12. Talent Wheel of Servant Leadership (Coetzer 2018b)

7.1.1   The athlete-transformation phase

The first development phase of the Talent Wheel of Servant Leadership is the athlete-transformation phase. In this phase, leaders transform employees into 'athletes', in other words, equip employees with the characteristics and competence associated with the athlete-leadership function, so that they are able to apply the objectives of the athlete-leadership function effectively in the workplace. The athlete-transformation phase consists of two steps, namely (1) to translate the higher-purpose vision of the organization by applying the soldier-leadership function and (2) to align, care for, and grow employees by applying the farmer-leadership function. This is explained below.

7.1.1.1 Step 1: Translate the higher-purpose vision

In this step, the leader translates the higher-purpose vision of the organization into a unit strategy and employee goals by applying the soldier-leadership function. This will make the higher-purpose vision practical for employees and make their work meaningful and their contribution clear. The aim of this step is to establish positional goals in line with the higher-purpose vision of the company. One way to translate the higher-purpose vision of the company into a unit strategy is to conduct a strategic workshop. During this workshop, employees determine how their work unit can support the achievement of the higher-purpose vision of the organization. Once a work-unit strategy has been established, employee or positional goals are set. The Strategic Alignment Matrix discussed in Chapter 3 can be used in this step to summarize the unit strategy and positional goals in one matrix.

The desired outcome of Step 1 in the athlete-transformation phase is translation of the higher-purpose vision into a work unit strategy and set goals for each position or employee that support the higher-purpose vision of the company.

7.1.1.2 Step 2: Align, care for, and grow the employee

The second step in the athlete-transformation phase is to align, care for, and grow the employee by applying the farmer-leadership function.

This step consists of six development goals, namely to (1) discover the life purpose, talents, knowledge, and skills of the employee, (2) create an effective work climate and culture to activate individual potential, talent, and engagement, (3) equip the employee with the knowledge, skills, and experience to manage his or her mental, emotional, and physical state, (4) establish a Personal Development Plan for each employee, (5) assist the employee to portray his or her true identity, (6) equip the employee with the knowledge, skills, and habit to purposefully self-reflect, and to (7) create awareness of important company policies and procedures, business ethics, and relevant legislation.

The first development goal in Step 2 is to help the employee discover his or her life purpose, talents, knowledge, and skills, which will create self-knowledge (the first objective of the athlete-leadership function). Ways to discover an individual's knowledge, skills, and talents are to (a) use psychometric and other assessments, (b) conduct an interview with the employee, and to use the (c) Personal Career Plan Guide (discussed in Chapter 6). Employee coaching sessions might also be useful to discover the employee's life purpose and talents and to finalize a Career Plan for the individual.

Once an employee's life purpose, talents, knowledge, and skills have been discovered, the leader and the employee need to craft a job for the employee, in line with the higher-purpose vision of the organization. Job crafting refers to the process in which the employee and the leader decide how best to apply the employee's talents, knowledge, and skills, in line with the life purpose of the individual and the higher-purpose vision of the organization. The desired development outcome is therefore alignment of the employee's talent, knowledge, skills, and life purpose with positional goals that were set in the previous step. In this way, the best-fit employee is allocated to a position or goal.

The second development goal in Step 2 of the athlete-transformation phase is to create a conducive work climate and culture to activate individual potential, talent, and engagement levels. The resources provided in Chapter 6 can be used in this step to create an effective climate and culture for the employee. For example, a leader can use climate and culture diagnostic surveys to evaluate the current work climate and culture in the work unit. A leader can then use the diagnostic results to identify any improvement areas and to establish and implement relevant interventions to improve the current work climate and culture for the employee. Additional resources that are useful in this step are, for example, the Employee Diagnostic Form and the Leader Approach Guides (also discussed in Chapter 6). The Employee Diagnostic Form can be used to diagnose the level of energy, motivation, and competence of the employee and to determine what the employee needs to flourish. The Leader Approach Guides can then be applied to meet the employee's specific needs. The desired development outcome is therefore a conducive work climate and a culture that enhances the employee's work engagement.

The third development goal of this step is to equip the employee with the knowledge, skills, and experience to manage his or her mental, emotional, and physical state. This will enhance self-management — the second objective of the athlete-leadership function. Ways to enhance the employee's ability to manage his or her mental state is to enroll the employee for neuro-leadership training and coaching. Such training will equip the employee with the methods and tactics to manage personal thoughts by building effective neuropaths, in order to become more productive and effective. The Thought Process Map (discussed in Chapter 4) can also be used in this step to help the employee form new neuropaths and to adopt more effective behavior. The employee can furthermore be enrolled on emotional intelligence training and coaching sessions, which will equip the employee with the skills to manage his or her emotional state effectively. Physical health checks would create awareness of the employee's current physical state, and a diet and exercise plan will help the employee to manage his or her physical state, enabling optimum performance. The Work–Life Satisfaction Wheel (described in Chapter 4) could, in addition, be useful in this step to determine the employee's current work–life satisfaction and to establish personal goals and actions to optimize the employee's work–life balance. The desired development outcome in this phase is an employee who is able to manage his or her mental, emotional, and physical state.

The fourth development goal of Step 2 in transforming the employee into an 'athlete' is to establish a Personal Development Plan for the employee. This will address the third objective of the athlete-leadership function, namely self-improvement. The leader could have an informal discussion with the employee to determine his or her development needs, and could use the Personal Development Plan Guide (discussed in Chapter 6) to establish a Personal Development Plan for the employee. The desired development outcome is implementation of a Personal Development Plan for the employee, in line with his or her life purpose, potential, and talents, as well as the higher-purpose vision of the organization.

The fifth development goal in Step 2 of the athlete-transformation phase is to assist the employee to portray his or her true identity without comparing him- or herself to others. This self-revelation is the fourth objective of the athlete-leadership function. During the alignment process, the employee became aware of his or her strengths, talents, and life purpose, which were then aligned to a specific goal, position, or task. The employee should now apply his or her personal uniqueness to achieve the higher-purpose vision of the organization. One way to help the employee to become more authentic is to enroll the employee for an individuality and authenticity workshop. A leader should, furthermore, encourage and help the employee to be authentic and to portray his or her true identity in the workplace, and to use his or her personal uniqueness to achieve the higher-purpose vision of the company.

The sixth development goal of Step 2 in the athlete-transformation phase is to equip the employee with the knowledge and skills to purposefully self-reflect, and to make it a habit. This will achieve the fifth objective of the athlete-leadership function, namely self-reflection. Self-reflection training and coaching could be useful to equip the employee with the knowledge, resources, and techniques to effectively self-reflect. The Self-reflection Guide (discussed in Chapter 4) could also be useful in this regard. The desired development outcome in this case is an employee who effectively and regularly self-reflects.

The seventh development goal of Step 2 in the athlete-transformation phase is to create awareness amongst employees of important company policies and procedures, business ethics, and relevant legislation. This achieves the sixth objective of the athlete-leadership function, namely employees staying within the rules. Training on company policy and procedure, business ethics, and relevant legislation is required to make the employee aware of current and new rules and regulations, and to equip him or her with the knowledge to abide by these. The training methods that could be used include electronic learning, classroom learning, or blended learning methods. The desired development outcome is an employee who abides by company policies and procedures and legislation while upholding business ethics.

A graphical display of the two steps in the athlete-transformation phase is provided in Figure 13. The development process of the athlete-transformation phase is also summarized in Table 17. This table provides a summary of the development goals, methods, and outcomes of the two steps of the athlete-transformation phase.

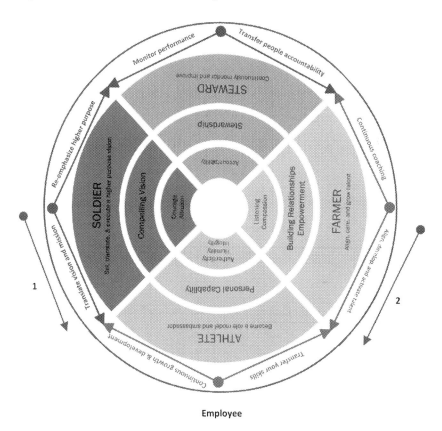

Figure 13. The athlete-transformation phase (Coetzer 2018b)

Table 17. Development process of the athlete-transformation phase

Development step	Development goal	Development method	Development outcome
Translate the higher-purpose vision for the employee	Establish positional goals in line with the higher-purpose vision of the organization	Strategic workshop Strategic Alignment Matrix	Positional goals and Key Performance Indicators (KPIs) in line with the higher-purpose vision of the organization
2.1 Align the employee	Self-knowledge: • Discover the life purpose, talents, knowledge, and skills of the employee	• Psychometric and other assessments • Employee interviews • Coaching sessions • Personal Career Plan Guide • Job-crafting workshop	The life purpose, talent, knowledge, and skills of an employee are successfully aligned to positional goals
2.2 Care for the employee	Create a conducive work climate and culture to activate individual potential, talent, and engagement	• Climate and culture assessments • Climate and culture feedback workshop • Climate and culture intervention • Employee Diagnostic Form • Leader Approach Guides	A conducive work climate and culture that increase the employee's level of work engagement

2.3 Grow the employee			
	Self-management: • Equip the employee with the knowledge, skills, and experience to manage his or her mental, emotional, and physical state	• Neuro-leadership training and coaching • Emotional intelligence training and coaching • Physical health check • Diet and exercise plan • Work–Life Satisfaction Wheel diagnosis and action plan	Employee is capable of managing his or her mental, emotional, and physical state
	Self-improvement: • Create a Personal Development Plan for the employee	• Discussion with employee on personal development • Personal Development Plan Guide	A Personal Development Plan for the employee, in line with his or her life purpose, potential, and talents, as well as the higher-purpose vision of the organization
	Self-revelation: • Assist the employee to portray his or her true identity	• Individuality and authenticity workshop	Employee is authentic in his or her dealings with others
	Self-reflection: • Equip the employee with the knowledge and skills to purposefully self-reflect and to make it a habit	• Self-reflection training and coaching • Self-reflection Guide	Employee is able to self-reflect effectively and regularly
	Stay within the rules: • Create awareness of important company policies and procedures, business ethics, and relevant legislation	• Training on company policies and procedures • Training on business ethics • Training on relevant legislation	Employee abides by company policies and procedures and relevant legislation, and upholds business ethics

7.1.2 The farmer-transformation phase

At the end of the athlete-transformation phase, the Talent Wheel of Servant Leadership rotates clockwise, and the leader then aims to make the employee a 'farmer'. The farmer-transformation phase consists of two steps, namely to (1) transfer the leader's people management skills to the employee by applying the athlete-leadership function and to (2) transfer some form of people accountability to the employee by applying the steward-leadership function.

7.1.2.1 Step 1: Transfer people-management skills

The first step in transforming an employee into a farmer is the leader transferring people management skills to the employee by applying the athlete-leadership function, namely to be a role model to the employee. The first development goal of this step is to equip the employee with the skill to align the life purpose, talents, knowledge, and skills of others to the higher-purpose vision of the organization.

In the previous phase, the employee was exposed to the alignment process to align his or her own life purpose, knowledge, skills, and talents to the higher-purpose vision of the organization. In this development phase, the employee is equipped to be able to perform this alignment process with others. The employee could be enrolled for an alignment workshop where he or she will receive the knowledge and tools to perform this alignment. Thereafter, the leader must create opportunities for the employee to practice this skill in the workplace by means of on-the-job training or experiential assignments. During and after these assignments, the leader must mentor the employee and provide constructive feedback on what the employee did well and how he or she could improve. Mentoring is thus required until the employee masters this skill. The desired development outcome in this regard is an employee who is able to align the life purpose, talent, knowledge and skills of others to the higher-purpose vision of the organization, which is the first objective of the farmer-leadership function.

The second development goal of Step 1 of the farmer-transformation phase is to equip the employee with the knowledge, skills, and experience to care for others by creating a conducive work climate and culture in which they will flourish. This represents the second objective of the farmer-leadership function: to care for and protect others. Ways to equip the employee may be to enroll the employee for training on organizational climate and culture, that he or she may gain knowledge of how to create a conducive work climate and culture in a work unit that would enhance the work engagement levels of employees. Thereafter, a leader must give the employee experiential assignments to apply the knowledge in the workplace. The desired development outcome is an employee who is able to create a conducive work climate and culture that enhance the work engagement levels of others.

The third development goal of Step 1 in the farmer-transformation phase is to equip the employee with the knowledge and skills to grow others effectively, which is the third objective of the farmer-leadership function. The first skill an individual requires to grow others successfully is the ability to coach others. Neuro-leadership and mentorship training might be beneficial in equipping the employee with this skill. The employee also needs the ability to create a Personal Development Plan for others. An employee should first attend a personal development plan workshop to become proficient at creating Personal Development Plans for others. Such a workshop could include the application of the Personal Development Plan Guide (discussed in Chapter 4). Once the employee has completed the workshop, the leader should invite the employee to shadow coaching, mentoring, and personal development planning sessions, to observe how an experienced leader applies these skills. Thereafter, the leader must create on-the-job training opportunities for the employee to practice the new skill in the workplace. Lastly, the leader should schedule regular mentoring sessions with the employee, to provide feedback and to further guide the employee to successfully apply this skill in the workplace. The desired outcome of these development activities is an employee who is able to effectively coach, mentor, and develop others.

7.1.2.2 Step 2: Transfer people accountability

The second step in the farmer-transformation phase is to transfer people accountability to the employee. In this step, the employee needs practical and formal experience to align, care for, and grow other employees. The leader transfers this accountability by applying the stewardship-leadership function of continuously monitoring and improving.

Periodical job rotation might be useful to give an employee practical experience in leading others. During this period, a leader must monitor the performance and progress of the employee closely. Team-leadership assignments could also be helpful. For example, the leader might ask the employee to lead a small project and to act as the team leader for the duration of the project. The leader must provide regular feedback and guidance to the employee by means of mentoring sessions, to ensure the employee succeeds in the job rotation or team-leadership assignments. The development outcome is an employee who is able to lead a team effectively.

A graphical display of the two steps in the farmer-transformation phase is provided in Figure 14. The development process of the farmer-transformation phase is summarized in Table 18.

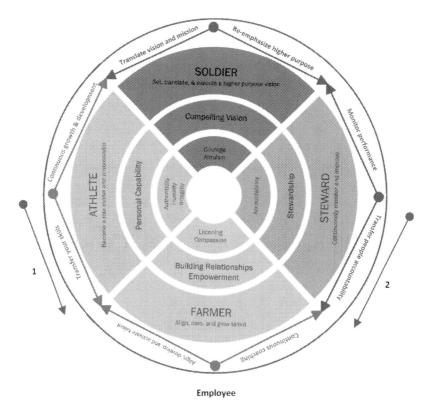

Figure 14. The farmer-transformation phase (Coetzer 2018b)

Table 18. Development process of the farmer-transformation phase

Development step	Development goal	Development method	Development outcome
1. Transfer your skills	Equip the employee with the knowledge, skills, and experience to align the life purpose, talents, knowledge, and skills of others to the higher-purpose vision of the organization	• Alignment workshop • On-the-job training • Mentoring sessions	Employee is able to align the life purpose, talents, knowledge, and skills of others to the higher-purpose vision of the organization
	Equip the employee with the knowledge and skills to care for others by creating a conducive work climate and culture in which others will flourish	• Training on organizational climate and culture • Experiential assignments	Employee is able to create a conducive work climate and culture that enhance the work engagement levels of others
	Equip the employee with the knowledge and skills to grow others effectively	• Neuro-leadership coaching training • Mentorship training • Personal Development Plan workshop • Shadowing • On-the-job training • Mentoring sessions	Employee is able to coach, mentor, and develop others
2. Transfer people accountability	Transfer people accountability to the employee	• Job rotation • Team-leadership assignments • Mentoring sessions	Employee is capable of leading a team effectively

7.1.3   The steward-transformation phase

Once the employee has completed the farmer-transformation phase, the Talent Wheel of Servant Leadership again rotates clockwise, and the leader then focuses on transforming the employee into a 'steward'. This phase includes two steps, namely to (1) develop, coach, and mentor the employee by applying the farmer-leadership function and to (2) re-emphasize the higher-purpose vision of the company by applying the soldier-leadership function.

7.1.3.1 Step 1: Continuous development, coaching, and mentoring

In this step, the leader continuously develops, coaches, and mentors the employee by applying the famer-leadership function. By equipping the employee with the knowledge, skills, and experience, the leader aims to achieve three development goals, namely to enable the employee (1) to apply good stewardship, (2) monitor the performance of others, and to (3) to improve policies, procedures, business processes and systems.

The first development goal of this step is to equip the employee with the knowledge, skills, and experience to apply good stewardship, which will enable the employee to implement the first objective of the steward-leadership function. This can be done by providing the employee with the Personal and Employer Stewardship Guides (described in Chapter 5) and to show the employee how to use these guides to review stewardship outcomes and to compile a Stewardship Plan. A leader must then ask the employee to implement Stewardship plans in his or her work unit, and schedule regular follow-up mentoring and coaching sessions with the employee, to guide him or her to achieve the stewardship objectives. The desired outcome of these development activities is an employee who is able to apply good stewardship.

The second development goal of Step 1 of the steward-transformation phase is to equip the employee with the knowledge, skills, and experience to monitor the performance of others, which is the second objective of the steward-leadership function. It could be helpful to send the employee for performance management training focused on (a) the importance of performance management, (b) the process of performance management, and (c) methods to apply performance management effectively in the workplace. The performance management system, policies, and procedures of the company should also be explained to the employee during the training session. After the employee has completed the initial performance management training, he or she must shadow the leader in performance management sessions, to observe how an experienced leader conducts (a) a performance goal-setting session, (b) a performance check-in session, and (c) a performance review session. Thereafter, the leader can task the employee to complete experiential assignments to apply his or her performance management knowledge. For example, the leader could task the employee with conducting a performance goal-setting session under the supervision of the leader. It is important that the leader provide constructive feedback to the employee during this process. Once the leader feels comfortable that the employee possesses the knowledge and skill to monitor the performance of others, the leader could ask the employee to implement the performance management system of the company in the employee's work unit. The leader should continue to provide constructive feedback, coaching, and mentoring to the employee, until the employee can apply performance management practices on his or her own. The desired outcome is an employee who is able to monitor the performance of others effectively.

The third development goal of Step 1 in the steward-transformation phase is to equip the employee with the knowledge, skills, and experience to improve policies, procedures, and business processes and systems, which will equip the employee to achieve the third objective of the steward-leadership function: to continuously improve. This could be done by inviting the employee to observe an improvement workshop in which a current policy, procedure, system, or business process is reviewed and actions are initiated to improve these, in line with the higher-purpose vision of the organization. Once an employee has participated in an improvement workshop, the leader should give the employee a relevant experiential assignment in the company. A leader could even task the employee with facilitating an improvement workshop. Continuous mentoring must form part of this process. The desired outcome of these activities is an employee who is able to improve policies, procedures, systems, and business processes.

7.1.3.2 *Step 2: Re-emphasize the higher-purpose vision*

The aim of this step of the steward-transformation phase is to re-emphasize the higher-purpose vision of the company. At this stage, the employee has started to lead others and to complete more advanced tasks. It is therefore important that the leader re-emphasize the higher-purpose vision of the company, to ensure the employee does not become prideful or abuse his or her power to achieve selfish objectives. The development goal here is to ensure the employee's intent originates from a heart of love and purpose, and that the motivation to perform is in line with the higher-purpose vision of the organization. This can be done by using 360-degree surveys to evaluate the leader-heart type of the employee. Such surveys provide useful information on how subordinates, colleagues, superiors, and even customers experience the leadership behavior of the employee. The leader must review the assessment results and provide constructive feedback to the employee. Another way to re-emphasize the higher-purpose vision is to review an employee's stewardship progress, in other words, to review the return on investment the employee produced and whether it is in line with the higher-purpose vision of the organization. The desired outcome is that the employee's intent originates from a loving and purposeful heart and the employee's intent to perform is in line with the higher-purpose vision of the company.

The two steps of the steward-transformation phase are presented in Figure 15. Table 19 provides a summary of the development goals, methods, and desired outcomes of the steward-leadership transformation phase.

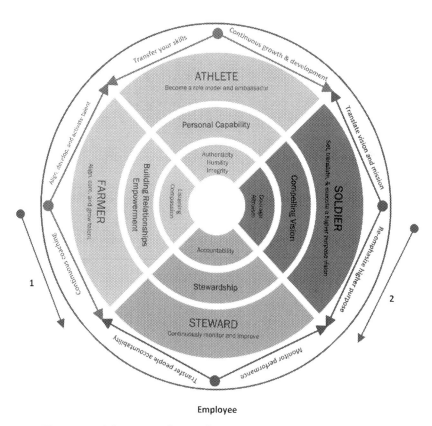

Figure 15. The steward-transformation phase (Coetzer 2018b)

Table 19. Development process of the steward-transformation phase

Development step	Development goal	Development method	Development outcome
1. Continuous development, mentoring, and coaching	Equip the employee with the knowledge, skills, and experience to apply good stewardship	• Stewardship Plan • Mentoring and coaching sessions	Employee is able to apply good stewardship
	Equip the employee with the knowledge, skills, and experience to monitor the performance of others	• Performance management workshop • Performance management shadowing • Performance management experiential assignments • Performance management implementation	Employee is able to monitor the performance of others effectively
	Equip the employee with the knowledge, skills, and experience to improve policies, procedures, and business processes and systems	• Improvement workshop • Experiential improvement assignments • Mentoring sessions	Employee is able to improve systems, processes, policies, procedures, and systems
2. Re-emphasize the higher-purpose vision	Ensure the employee's intent is in line with the higher-purpose vision of the organization	• Evaluate the employee's leader-heart type and provide feedback • Evaluate stewardship progress (return on investment in terms of the higher-purpose vision of the organization)	Employee's intent originates from a loving heart and is in line with the higher-purpose vision of the organization

7.1.4 *The soldier-transformation phase*

After the employee has completed the steward-transformation phase, the Talent Wheel of Servant Leadership once again rotates clockwise, and the leader then aims to transform the employee into a 'soldier', in other words, to equip the employee to apply the soldier-leadership function. This phase consists of two steps, namely (1) to monitor the performance of the employee continuously by applying the steward-leadership function and (2) to continuously grow and develop the employee by transferring the leader's skills through the athlete-leadership function.

7.1.4.1 *Step 1: Monitor performance*

The first step in this phase is for the leader to monitor the performance of the employee by applying the steward-leadership function. This step consists of two development goals, namely (1) to review the performance of the employee and (2) to establish or update the unit strategy and employee goals, in line with the higher-purpose vision of the organization.

The first development goal of this step is to review the performance of the employee and the work unit to determine the contribution of the employee and the team towards achieving the higher-purpose vision of the organization. This is done by means of individual and team performance review sessions. The leader and the work team must review the team's performance against the higher-purpose vision of the company and identify any improvement areas. The leader should also conduct individual performance sessions with the employee, to review his or her performance against the higher-purpose vision of the company. The leader and the employee must also identify any individual improvement areas. The desired outcome of these activities is a review of the performance of the employee and the work unit, and identification of any improvement areas.

The second development goal of Step 1 in the soldier-transformation phase is to establish or update the unit strategy and employee goals, in line with the higher-purpose vision of the organization. The leader should invite the employee to participate in strategic workshops in which the work unit strategy and positional goals are updated (or established, if a unit strategy does not currently exist), to support the higher-purpose vision of the company. This will give the employee practical experience in translating the higher-purpose vision of the company into a work-unit strategy. The desired outcome is an updated unit strategy and employee goals, in line with the higher-purpose vision of the company.

7.1.4.2 Step 2: Grow and develop the employee

This step in the soldier-transformation phase requires of the leader to grow and develop the employee by teaching him or her and by transferring expert skills. This step consists of two development goals, namely (1) to equip the employee with the knowledge, skills, and experience to set, translate, and execute a higher-purpose vision and (2) to identify any additional development goals for the employee to update the employee's Personal Development Plan.

The first development goal of Step 2 of the soldier-transformation phase is to equip the employee with the knowledge, skills, and experience to set, translate, and execute a higher-purpose vision. This can be done by enrolling the employee for strategy-alignment training in which the knowledge and application tools are transferred to the employee to enable him or her to develop a work-unit strategy that supports the higher-purpose vision of the organization. Application of the Strategic Alignment Matrix (discussed in Chapter 3) could be included in this training. Once an employee has completed the initial training, the leader must give the employee experiential assignments to apply the knowledge in the workplace. For example, the leader might ask the employee to establish a work-unit strategy for a small unit or department in the company. The leader must also schedule regular mentoring sessions with the employee, and mentor and guide the employee in successfully completing the experiential assignments. The desired outcome of these development activities is an employee who is able to set, translate, and execute a higher-purpose vision.

A second development goal in this step is to identify any additional development goals for the employee and to update the employee's Personal Development Plan. The leader should schedule a one-on-one session with the employee to discuss additional personal development areas of the employee and to plan personal development actions to activate the employee's talent and potential, in line with the life purpose of the employee and the higher-purpose vision of the organization. The leader could also use the Personal Development Plan Guide (in Chapter 6) in this session, to establish a new Personal Development Plan for the employee. The desired outcome in this instance is identification of any additional development areas for the employee and an updated Personal Development Plan for the employee.

A graphical display of the two steps in the soldier-transformation phase is provided in Figure 16, and the development process of the soldier-transformation phase is summarized in Table 20.

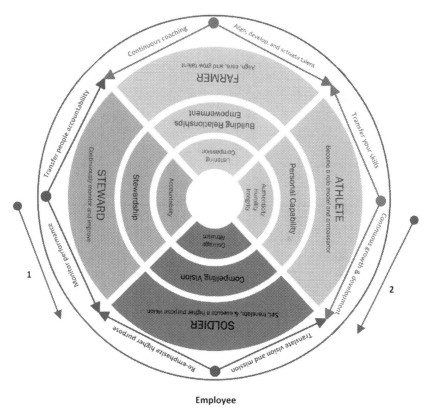

Figure 16. The soldier-transformation phase (Coetzer 2018b)

Table 20. Development process of the soldier-transformation phase

Development step	Development goal	Development method	Development outcome
1. Monitor performance	Review performance on achieving employee- and work unit goals in line with the higher-purpose vision of the organization	• Performance review sessions of employee's goals • Performance review sessions of the work-unit's strategy	Performance of employee and work unit has been reviewed and improvement areas identified, to achieve the higher-purpose vision of the organization
	Establish or update the unit strategy and employee's goals in line with the higher-purpose vision of the organization	• Reiterate the higher-purpose vision of the organization • Review the unit strategy and employee's goals to ensure alignment with the higher-purpose vision of the organization • Participate in strategic workshop	Employee goals and unit strategy are aligned with the higher-purpose vision of the organization
2. Continuous growth and development	Equip the employee with the knowledge, skills, and experience to set, translate, and execute a higher-purpose vision	• Strategic alignment workshop • Strategic Alignment Matrix • Experiential assignment • Mentoring and coaching sessions	Employee is able to set, translate, and execute a higher-purpose vision
	Identify additional development goals and update employee's Personal Development Plan	• Personal development discussion • Personal Development Plan Guide	Employee development needs identified and Employee Development Plan updated

7.2 Framework for Effective Servant-leadership Development

The second framework to develop servant-leaders proposes five formal phases and incorporates the barriers to and antecedents of servant-leadership development (Coetzer 2018b). The five phases of effective servant-leadership development are: (1) identification, (2) evaluation, (3) development, (4) embedment, and (5) impact. These phases are applicable for the implementation of a formal servant leadership development program within an organization.

The five development phases are clustered into three time frames, namely before-learning, during-learning, and after-learning. The identification and evaluation phases fall within the before-learning time frame, the development phase falls within the during-learning time frame, and the embedment and impact phases fall within the after-learning time frame. The Framework for Effective Servant-leadership Development also includes the type of support that a participating employee requires from his or her direct manager or leader in each development phase. A summary of this framework is presented in Figure 17.

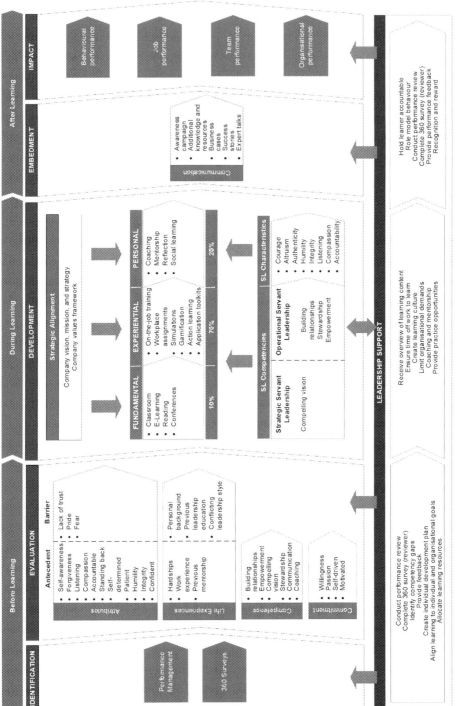

Figure 17. Framework for Effective Servant-leadership Development (Coetzer 2018b)

7.2.1   Identification

The first phase in the framework to effectively develop servant-leaders is identification. This phase is implemented before a formal learning program starts. Identification refers to the process of identifying potential servant-leaders in the organization. Two methods can be used to identify these employees, namely performance review records and 360-degree surveys. During the informal development process — the implementation of the Talent Wheel of Servant Leadership — the leader worked on a one-on-one basis with the employee to transform him or her into a servant-leader and regularly reviewed the employee's performance. These performance review records can be used in the formal process to identify whether a person has the potential and desire to be promoted to a leadership position in the organization.

A 360-degree survey is another method organizations can use to identify potential future leaders. In this survey, the employee, subordinates, colleagues, and superiors evaluate the leadership behavior and practices of a person. An example of a 360-degree survey is the Heartstyles Indicator (Anderson & Jahng 2014). This survey measures the leader-heart type of a person from the perspective of the employee, as well as from the perspective of others (subordinates, colleagues, superiors). The results of this survey indicate whether a person leads from a heart of love and humility or from a heart of fear and pride. As discussed in Chapter 2, the heart of a leader is the most important dimension of servant leadership, as leadership behavior originates from a person's intent. Knowledge, ability, and skills are also applied in accordance with a person's heart intent. A servant-leader leads from a loving heart; therefore, employees who show a loving heart in this survey should be identified as potential servant-leaders.

To support an employee during the identification phase, the leader should (a) have the employee complete a 360-degree survey to evaluate the employee's leadership behavior, (b) conduct performance reviews with the employee to determine performance intent, and (c) provide constructive feedback to the employee and identify individual strengths and development areas.

7.2.2 Evaluation

The second phase that must be implemented before a formal learning program commences is evaluation. This is the process of evaluating the personal antecedents and barriers that could either promote or hinder the employee's servant-leadership development. Research indicates that servant-leadership development is hindered by personal barriers such as certain personal attributes and life experiences, and by organizational barriers such as organizational demands, lack of leadership support, and constant change (Coetzer 2018b). Servant-leadership development is promoted by personal antecedents such as certain personal attributes, competence, life experiences, and commitment, and by organizational antecedents such as development opportunities, leadership support, performance management, 360-degree surveys, communication, strategic alignment, and organizational culture (Coetzer 2018b). It is therefore important to evaluate these barriers and antecedents on a personal level, in order to customize the employee's leadership development. This will enhance the probability of the employee adopting servant leadership and increase the effectiveness of the servant-leadership development program.

The personal attributes that promote servant-leadership development are self-awareness, forgiveness, listening, compassion, accountability, standing back, self-determination, patience, humility, integrity, and confidence (Coetzer 2018b). The personal attributes that hinder servant-leadership development are lack of trust, pride, and fear (Coetzer 2018b). These personal attributes should be evaluated to determine a person's strengths and development areas, before learning starts. A servant-leadership development program could then be customized to build on the personal attributes that will promote servant-leadership behavior and to bridge those attributes that will hinder the adoption of servant-leadership behavior.

The life experiences that promote servant-leadership development are hardships, work experience, and previous servant-leadership mentoring (Coetzer 2018b). In other words, when an individual has experienced hardship in his or her life, has ample work experience, and has had a servant-leader as mentor, the probability of the individual adopting servant-leadership behavior is greater. However, there are also life experiences that could hinder servant-leadership development, such as personal background and upbringing, previous leadership education, and a current, conflicting leadership style. These types of life experiences should thus also be evaluated, to determine if they could hamper the individual's servant-leadership development. Development programs can then be modified to build on life experiences that promote servant-leadership behavior and to overcome life experiences that hinder servant-leadership behavior.

Research also indicates that a person's ability to (a) build relationships, (b) empower others, (c) set a compelling vision, (d) apply good stewardship, (e) communicate well, and (f) coach others promote the probability of servant-leadership development (Coetzer 2018b). A person's level of competence should thus be evaluated in terms of these competencies, to determine a person's strengths and development areas, before embarking on a formal development program. One way to evaluate a person's competence is to give the employee experiential assignments and then evaluate his or her competence during and after the assignments. Most of these competencies were also developed in the informal development process using the Talent Wheel of Servant Leadership. If a leader completed the informal development process with the employee (applied the Talent Wheel of Servant Leadership), he or she should have enough evidence to determine an employee's level of competence to build relationships, empower others, apply good stewardship, communicate well with others, coach others, and to set a compelling vision. However, formal competence assessments are still recommended to determine a person's current competence in these areas. After evaluation, a servant-leadership development program can be individualized to focus more on the competencies on which the employee scored low.

Another factor that could promote servant-leadership development is the level of commitment of the individual (Coetzer 2018b). This refers to the person's willingness, passion, self-determination, and motivation to become a servant-leader and to complete a servant-leadership development program. The level of individual commitment should thus be evaluated to determine the probability of the employee (a) actively participating in the program, (b) completing all program activities, (c) adopting servant-leader behavior, and (d) diligently practicing and implementing the program content.

The leadership support required for the evaluation phase takes the form of several activities. The first activity is for the leader to evaluate the competence levels of the employee and identify any employee competency gaps. Thereafter, the leader should provide constructive feedback to the employee and establish a Personal Development Plan, together with the employee, in line with the individual's life purpose and the higher purpose of the organization. A direct manager or leader must furthermore allocate learning resources to the employee to complete the learning activities listed in the Personal Development Plan, for example, a training budget for the Personal Development Plan.

7.2.3   Development

The third phase in cultivating servant-leaders in an organization is formal development. This phase falls within the during-learning time frame. Development refers to actual learning activities to (a) transfer knowledge of what servant leadership is and how to apply it, (b) provide opportunities to practice servant leadership in the workplace, and to (c) initiate and cultivate personal transformation and adopt servant-leadership behavior.

The first aim in the development phase is to align a servant-leadership development program with the higher-purpose vision, mission, strategy, and values of the organization. Such alignment will ensure that the servant-leadership development program is delivered in accordance with the higher-purpose vision of the organization. Proper alignment of a development program will also make it easier for participating employees to apply the learning in their immediate work context. It is thus recommended that the higher-purpose vision for the organization be established before implementing a servant-leadership development program.

The Organizational Values Framework must also be aligned to the values of servant leadership before implementing a servant-leadership development program. A values alignment assignment can then be incorporated in the development program, in which individual values are aligned to the values of servant leadership and to the values of the organization. Such an assignment will help individuals to become more aware of unknown strengths or blind spots regarding their personal values, and could also help them to plan and implement personal development actions to align their personal values and behavior to the values of servant leadership and to the values of the organization.

The second aim of the development phase is to design a servant-leadership development program that incorporates fundamental, experiential, and personal transformation learning activities. Fundamental learning activities are activities such as classroom training, electronic learning, reading, or conferences that transfer foundational knowledge to the employee. Experiential learning activities are activities or resources to apply learning in the workplace, such as on-the-job training, workplace assignments, simulations, gamification, action learning, and application toolkits. Personal learning activities aim to cultivate personal transformation, and include learning activities such as coaching, mentoring, reflection, and social learning.

Literature suggests that development programs should consist of 10% fundamental learning activities, 70% experiential learning activities, and 20% personal transformation learning activities (Lombardo & Eichinger 2006). Learning will be more sustainable over time if a variety of learning activities are included in a development program of which the majority of activities are experiential.

Leadership-development training often requires behavioral change, which cannot take place in short programs. The human brain needs time, practice, and consistent focus to develop new neuropaths in order to master a skill or behavior. Leadership-development practitioners should therefore use a micro-learning approach in designing servant-leadership development programs, and include a variety of short fundamental, experiential, and personal learning activities that are completed over a longer time frame. Knowledge is then transferred, applied, and experienced in portions, over a longer period, which will sustain learning.

A servant-leadership development program should, furthermore, emphasize the characteristics and competencies of a servant-leader. Servant leadership is characterized by courage, altruism, authenticity, listening, humility, integrity, compassion, and accountability, as well as the competencies of setting a compelling vision, personal capability, empowerment, building relationships, and stewardship (Coetzer et al. 2017). A servant-leadership development program should thus enhance servant-leadership characteristics and competencies, and enable individuals to apply these behaviors and skills effectively in the workplace.

The type of leadership support a direct manager should provide to a participating employee during the development phase is to (1) review the learning content, (2) ensure time off work to learn, (3) limit organizational demands, (4) create a learning culture, (5) provide coaching and mentoring, and (6) provide practice opportunities.

Before an employee starts a servant-leadership development program, his or her direct manager or leader must receive an overview of the context, aim, content, and structure of a servant-leadership development program. This will enable the manager to support the employee in completing the program. It might even be beneficial for executive or senior management to first complete the servant-leadership development program before middle or junior managers complete the same program. Senior leaders will then fully understand the content, purpose, and structure of the program, and will be better able to support their direct reports.

Another type of support a direct manager should provide to a participating employee is to plan work in such a way that the employee has time to complete the learning activities of the program. Often, employees are unable to complete the learning activities of a servant-leadership development program because they cannot afford to take time from their daily work schedule. Leaders should thus plan and allocate work in such a way that the employee is able to complete his or her work responsibilities as well as the learning activities of the program. During the program, direct managers should also limit organizational demands that might hinder a participating employee's timeous completion of the learning activities.

A direct manager must, furthermore, create a learning culture in the department or work unit under his or her supervision. A learning culture is one that promotes and encourages learning and continuous personal development. A leader could create such a culture by (a) encouraging employees to complete learning activities, (b) providing opportunities to apply the learning in the workplace, (c) becoming fully involved in the personal development of employees, (d) coaching and mentoring employees before and after learning, (e) ensuring learning is in line with the life purpose of the individual, the positional requirements of the employee, and the higher-purpose vision of the organization, (f) providing constructive reflection time, and by (g) evaluating the impact of learning on individual, team, and organizational performance.

Other practical ways to support an employee during the development phase is to coach the employee before and after learning activities, to mentor the employee, and to provide practice opportunities in the workplace to apply the learning. For example, after a classroom training session, the leader could schedule a coaching or mentoring session with the employee to understand what the employee learned and to help the employee apply the learning in the workplace. The leader could also create workplace assignments or simulations for the employee to implement the learning in the current context and then evaluate the employee's success. A key requirement of this process is creating an environment in which it is safe for the employee to make mistakes, as people often learn though failure. Reflection and mentoring during and after failure are, however, crucial in helping the employee successfully complete the experiential assignment in a next attempt.

7.2.4 Embedment

The fourth development phase is embedment, which is implemented after a formal development program. The purpose of this phase is to sustain learning after an employee has completed the servant-leadership development program, by implementing several continuous communication strategies. A first strategy to embed servant-leadership development is to implement awareness campaigns in the organization after a formal development program. Such campaigns could include corporate posters, articles, videos, corporate theaters, gifts, games or competitions, and social media campaigns.

Another way to embed servant-leadership learning is to create online knowledge centers. A knowledge center consists of articles, videos, resources, and application toolkits related to servant leadership. Employees can then access the online knowledge center and view and download additional resources to apply servant leadership in the workplace such as application toolkits, business case studies, research reports, articles, videos, books, guides, etc. An automated communication plan could also be embedded within a knowledge center, to send additional servant-leadership resources to employees on a regular and continuous basis. The knowledge center should be updated frequently to include new research, developments, and case studies related to servant leadership. The knowledge center could furthermore include continuous professional development (CPD) activities. A CPD scoring system could be established, where individuals need to complete a certain number of learning activities to achieve a minimum development score to maintain their leadership position or certification in the organization. In this way, employees continuously receive updated information regarding servant leadership.

A third method to embed servant leadership in an organization is to create and publish business cases within the organization. A business case is a summary of a real-life scenario where servant leadership was implemented and the impact thereof. Leaders should encourage employees to collect evidence on the impact of servant leadership in the current context after they completed a servant-leadership development program. The impact of servant leadership should be measured from the perspective of multiple stakeholders (customers, employees, shareholders, suppliers, society, and the environment). A good business case generally includes a pre- and post-assessment. For example, the level of customer service and satisfaction can be measured before a servant-leadership development program started, and then again after the program has been completed in the organization. The results of the pre-and post-assessments could then be compared, to determine the impact of servant leadership. Another example is to measure employee work engagement levels of employees before and after a leader completed the servant-leadership development program. The pre- and post-assessment can then be compared, to determine the impact of servant leadership on the work engagement levels of employees. Pre- and post-assessments could also be done to measure the impact of servant leadership on shareholder value, supplier relationships, and even the environment or society. Business cases should be communicated to all employees and leaders in the organization and should be added to the knowledge center.

A fourth way to embed servant-leadership is to record and communicate success stories from leaders who participated in the program. One way to communicate success stories in the organization is to video-record the experiences of employees during and after the servant-leadership development program and send it to employees via an internal communication platform. Another way to communicate success stories is to interview employees who participated in a servant-leadership development program and ask them to share their experiences in implementing servant leadership in the workplace and the impact thereof. The best stories can then be recognized and awarded. Employees who had participated in a servant-leadership development program could also share their experiences in article format in which they provide specific recommendations on how to implement servant leadership. These articles can then be published through the knowledge center.

A fifth way to embed servant-leadership development is to regularly invite experts to present a masterclass and share updated research on servant leadership. This will ensure that the organization's application of servant leadership remains current and relevant. Such masterclasses could be recorded, with the permission of the expert, and added to the knowledge center. Employees who could not attend the live session can then view the masterclass on the online knowledge center at any time. This method is similar to TED Talks, but is customized to the specific context of the organization.

7.2.5   Impact

The fifth development phase is to formally measure the impact of learning in terms of behavioral performance, job performance, team performance, and organizational performance. Behavioral performance refers to the change in leadership behavior and effectiveness after completing a servant-leadership development program. A 360-degree survey can be used to measure how the program improved the leadership behavior of an individual. For example, colleagues, superiors, and direct reports could complete a leadership survey before and after a person completed a servant-leadership development program. The results of the pre- and post-assessments can then be compared, to determine the impact of the learning on the leader's behavior.

The change in the employee's job performance must also be measured after completion of the program. The performance review process of the company can be used in this regard. A performance review should be conducted before and after the employee has completed the program, and the two reviews can then be compared, to determine the impact of the program. A discussion with the employee might be needed to understand which factors increased the person's job performance the most.

The impact of the learning on team performance should furthermore be measured. Specific team performance metrics could be established and measured before and after a team leader completed the servant-leadership development program. The comparison of the pre- and post-assessment results will then indicate any team performance improvements. Team performance measurements to determine the return on learning investment should be as specific and objective as possible.

The impact of learning on organizational performance should also be measured. Although many factors may influence organizational performance, leaders must find a way to measure this impact. For example, learning outcomes can be aligned to the strategic outcomes of the organization. A leader can then determine whether a learning program was effective in equipping employees with the required competencies to achieve the strategic objectives.

A specific measurement that could be useful in this regard is human capital return on investment (HCROI). This refers to how much profit a business generates in proportion to the human capital costs of the business, and is calculated as follows: Revenue – (Expenses – [Payroll bill + Benefits]) ÷ Payroll bill + Benefits (Viljoen & Kock 2012). This calculation can be done per division, department, or work unit before and after that area's leader completed a servant-leadership development program. The pre- and post-assessment results can then be compared.

Another use of the HCROI measurement is to compare the HCROI result of one division (in which the leaders completed the servant-leadership development program) versus another division (in which the leaders did not complete the program) over a fixed period, while limiting or controlling for other factors that might influence the results. This will provide a good indication of the return the servant-leadership development program yielded.

Additional metrics that can be used to measure the impact of a servant-leadership development program on organizational performance are customer satisfaction levels, supplier efficiency levels, employee's work engagement levels, productivity levels, employee turnover, financial return on investment (FROI), return on assets (ROA), profit, shareholder value, and environmental impact. It is important to also conduct a pre- and post-assessment to determine how a servant-leadership development program impacted organizational performance.

The type of leadership support required in the embedment and impact phases is for the leader to (a) hold the employee accountable for learning, (b) role model servant-leadership behavior, (c) conduct performance reviews, (d) participate in 360-degree survey reviews of the employee, (e) provide assessments and performance feedback to the employee, and (f) recognize and reward servant-leadership performance. Recognition and rewards, specifically, play a crucial role in embedding servant leadership in an organization. The organization must recognize and reward the effective application of servant-leadership behavior in the organization. A rating system in which 360-degree surveys, business cases, success stories, and individual, job, team, and organizational performance reviews are consolidated can be used to reveal the best servant-leaders in the organization. These top performers can then be rewarded and recognized at formal corporate events with appropriate recognition methods such as bonuses, extended leave, corporate gifts, or any other reward preferable to the employee.

7.3 Implementation of the two development frameworks

This chapter provided two frameworks to effectively develop servant-leaders in an organization. The Talent Wheel of Servant Leadership is an informal development process a leader initiates with an employee. This is a one-on-one approach to transform an employee into a servant-leader and to equip the employee to fulfil the four functions of servant leadership in the workplace. The Framework for Effective Servant-leadership Development is a formal development process that can be implemented to develop all leaders in the organization simultaneously and to cultivate a servant-leadership culture. It consists of five formal development phases, and incorporates the personal and organizational antecedents of or barriers to effective servant-leadership development.

The two processes or frameworks work together and complement each other in cultivating effective servant-leaders, and could be applied simultaneously or separately. One application could be to use the informal development process (the Talent Wheel of Servant Leadership) to identify potential leaders and then have them complete the formal development process (the Framework for Effectively Servant-leadership Development), before promoting them to leadership positions.

CHAPTER 8
A FRAMEWORK AND PROCEDURE TO IMPLEMENT SERVANT LEADERSHIP

Chapter 1 of this book emphasized a global leadership crisis, proposing that a different leadership approach is needed to sustain people, businesses, and society, now and in the future. Servant leadership seems to be the ideal leadership approach, as it starts with an intent to serve, operates from a people-first philosophy, and focuses on serving multiple stakeholders. Chapter 1 also highlighted that a leader's heart and intent are the main differentiators between a self-serving leader and a servant-leader. A servant-leader leads from a loving heart, whereas a self-serving leader leads from a prideful or fearful heart. In Chapter 2, the heart of a servant-leader was discussed, and Chapters 3 to 6 described the four functions of servant leadership. Two frameworks to develop servant-leaders were proposed in Chapter 7, namely the Talent Wheel of Servant Leadership and the Framework for Effective Servant-leadership Development.

In this chapter, the information of all the previous chapters is summarized in the Systematic Servant Leadership Model. A standard implementation procedure is also provided, which could be used in any organization.

8.1 The Systematic Servant Leadership Model

The Systematic Servant Leadership Model summarizes the functions of a servant-leader into one framework and suggests a systematic approach to apply the four functions in an organization (Coetzer 2018a). The Systematic Servant Leadership Model consists of five phases, namely to (1) apply the soldier-leadership function to set, translate, and execute a higher-purpose vision for the company, (2) apply the athlete-leadership function to become a role model and ambassador in the organization, (3) apply the farmer-leadership function to align, care for, and grow employees, (4) apply the steward-leadership function to monitor performance and to improve the products, services, policies, procedures, systems, and processes of the organization, and to (5) apply the Talent Wheel of Servant Leadership to transform employees into servant-leaders. The Systematic Servant Leadership Model is presented in Figure 18.

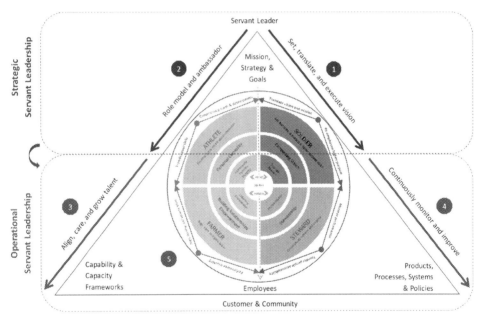

Figure 18. Systematic Servant Leadership Model (Coetzer 2018a)

8.1.1 Phase 1: Set, translate, and execute a higher-purpose vision

During this phase, a servant-leader applies the soldier-leadership function to set, translate, and execute a higher-purpose vision for the organization. A higher-purpose vision should be set from a loving leader-heart, and not from of a prideful or fearful leader-heart. If a higher-purpose vision is set from a prideful or fearful heart, the organization will focus on internal success, to the detriment of other stakeholders. However, if a higher-purpose vision is set from a loving heart, the organization will focus on creating value for multiple stakeholders, including customers, employees, shareholders, suppliers, society, and the environment.

Once a higher-purpose vision has been set, a leader needs to translate the higher-purpose vision into an organizational mission, strategy, and goals. An organizational mission, strategy, and goals should focus primarily on the customer and society, because that is why the organization exists, and secondarily on employees, because the employees are the closest to product production and to serving customers. A leader should, furthermore, develop the business processes, systems, policies, and procedures, as well as the Capability and Capacity Frameworks to support the higher-purpose vision, mission, strategy, and goals. A Capacity Framework refers to the type and number of positions required to execute the higher-purpose vision, mission, and strategy. A Capability Framework refers to the type of knowledge, skills, and attributes required to execute the higher-purpose vision, mission, and strategy of the organization. Employees should thereafter be aligned to the Capability and Capacity Frameworks, as well as the processes, systems, and policies of the company.

8.1.2 *Phase 2: Become a role model and ambassador*

Once a higher-purpose vision has been set and translated, a leader must apply the athlete-leadership function to become a role model and ambassador for the higher-purpose vision. During this phase, the leader focuses on enhancing personal leadership and capability to lead others to accomplish the higher-purpose vision. The leader thus applies the objectives of the athlete-leadership function in this phase, namely self-knowledge, self-management, self-improvement, self-revelation, self-reflection, and staying within the rules.

8.1.3 *Inverting the hierarchy*

During the first two phases of the Servant Leadership Model, the leader applies the *strategic* servant-leadership functions, namely the soldier-leadership function and the athlete-leadership function, to set and translate the higher-purpose vision for the organization and to become a role model and ambassador for that vision by leading him- or herself effectively. These two functions form part of the *head* dimension of servant leadership. Thereafter, the leader needs to invert the hierarchy before applying the operational servant-leadership functions, namely the farmer-leadership function and the steward-leadership function.

The inversion of the hierarchy is crucial and one of the main principles of servant leadership. If the hierarchy is not inverted, employees will serve leaders and the customers will suffer. However, when the hierarchy is inverted, leaders serve and empower employees to serve customers. This will ultimately result in achievement of the higher-purpose vision of the company, which focuses firstly on customers and society and secondly on employees.

In summary, a leader first applies his or her head (strategic servant-leadership functions) to set and translate a higher-purpose vision for the organization and to become a role model and ambassador for that vision, and then inverts the hierarchy to apply his or her hands (operational servant-leadership functions) to empower and support employees to accomplish the higher-purpose vision. Both the *head* (strategic leadership) and *hands* (operational leadership) dimensions are influence by the *heart* dimension (leadership intent and values). A servant-leader should thus apply strategic and operational leadership from a loving heart.

8.1.4   Phase 3: Align, care for, and grow employees

Once the hierarchy has been inverted, the leader initiates Phase 3 of the Systematic Servant Leadership Model: applying the farmer-leadership function to align, care for, and grow employees to achieve the higher-purpose vision. During this phase, the leader empowers and supports employees to execute the higher-purpose vision by applying the objectives of the farmer-leadership function.

The first step in this phase is to align the talents, life purpose, knowledge, skills, and attributes of employees to the higher-purpose vision, using the Capacity and Capability Frameworks established in Phase 1. In other words, employees are aligned to specific positions and roles, specified in the Capacity and Capability Frameworks, that support the higher-purpose vision of the organization. This will ensure good person–job and person–organization fit to execute the higher-purpose vision, mission, and strategy of the organization. Thereafter, the leader needs to create a conducive work climate and culture in the organization, in order to activate individual talent and potential in line with the higher-purpose vision. Leaders should furthermore establish Personal Development Plans for employees, to grow them continuously, in line with the Capability Framework of the organization and the life purpose of the individual.

8.1.5 Phase 4: Continuously monitor and improve

This phase of the Systematic Servant Leadership Model requires of the leader to apply the steward-leadership function to monitor performance and progress in accordance with the higher-purpose vision of the company, using the processes, systems, and policies established in Phase 1. In other words, the leader uses the business processes, systems, and policies to monitor, measure, and evaluate employee and organizational performance to determine the progress made towards achieving the higher-purpose vision, mission, and strategy.

A leader must also strive to continuously improve the processes, systems, policies, and procedures of the company, to ensure the organization operates at high efficiency and productivity levels, to achieve the higher-purpose vision of the company. The leaders should also review, update, and improve the company's products and services, to ensure these are relevant to the needs of customers and society. A leader must therefore continuously monitor and improve by applying the objectives of the steward-leadership function, namely to (a) apply good stewardship, (b) continuously monitor performance, and (c) continuously improve products, services, processes, systems, policies, and procedures.

8.1.6 Phase 5: Apply the Talent Wheel of Servant Leadership

Once the leader has applied all the servant-leadership functions, he or she needs to apply the informal development process of the Talent Wheel of Servant Leadership to transform employees into servant-leaders. The leader also uses this process to identify potential employees for future leadership positions in the company. Potential employees should then be enrolled on a formal development process, as proposed by the Framework for Effective Servant-leadership Development, before being promoted to a leadership position. In this way, the leader also prepares successors to take up future leadership positions as the organization grows.

8.2 A standard implementation procedure for servant leadership

A procedure to implement servant leadership in an organization is presented in Figure 19. This procedure consists of three phases, namely (1) Preparation, (2) Development, and (3) Sustainability.

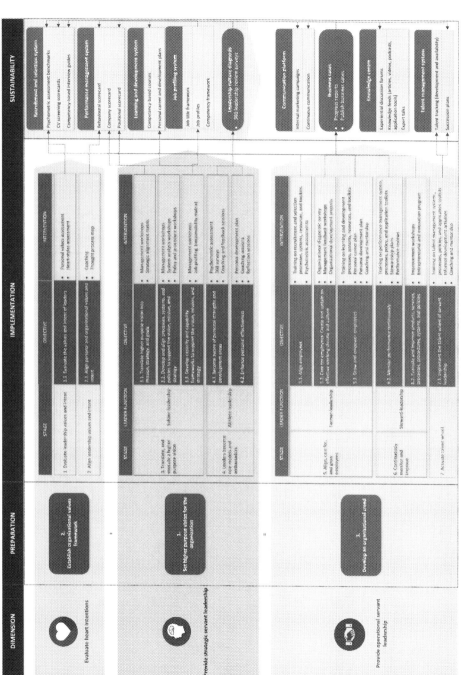

Figure 19. An implementation procedure for servant leadership

8.2.1 Phase 1: Preparation

The *Preparation* phase has three objectives: (1) set a higher-purpose vision for the organization, (2) establish the Organizational Values Framework, and (3) develop an organizational creed. These objectives should be completed before the *Implementation* phase.

8.2.1.1 Establish a higher-purpose vision

The **first objective** in the *Preparation* phase is to set a higher-purpose vision for the organization. As discussed in Chapter 3, a higher-purpose vision indicates how an organization creates value for multiple stakeholders, and describes (a) the purpose and intent of the organization, (b) how the organization's products and services serve society's needs, and (c) the type of legacy the organization desires to leave in the world.

It is important to involve multiple stakeholders in the process of setting a higher-purpose vision for the company, such as employees, shareholders, customers, and suppliers. Surveys and focus groups could be used to collect quantitative and qualitative data in this regard. For example, a Strategic Intent Survey could be sent to customers, employees, shareholders, and suppliers to determine (a) how the organization could create value for each stakeholder, now and in the future, (b) how each stakeholder perceives the strategic intent of the company, and to determine (c) the current and future needs of each stakeholder. Focus groups could, in addition, be valuable to collect qualitative data on the organization's purpose and intent. For instance, the main results of the quantitative surveys could be used as a basis to conduct focus groups with each stakeholder group, to gather qualitative insights on the survey results. The survey and focus group data could then be combined into a formal report to describe the needs, perspectives, and inputs of each stakeholder group. Thereafter, strategic workshop sessions could be scheduled with the leadership of the organization, who could then use the quantitative and qualitative data obtained from all the stakeholders to compile a higher-purpose vision for the organization. Once finalized, the leadership team should communicate the higher-purpose vision of the company to all stakeholders.

8.2.1.2 Establish the Organizational Values Framework

The **second objective** of the *Preparation* phase is to establish an Organizational Values Framework that supports the higher-purpose vision of the company. A values framework describes specific values and behaviors that are required to achieve the higher-purpose vision. Each company value should be clearly defined, and specific behaviors should be ascribed to the value. The behavioral indicators of each value can then be used to measure value-based behavior in the company. A bottom-up approach is appropriate for establishing company values, and a top-down approach is appropriate for implementing the values in the organization. A bottom-up approach refers to the process of getting the input of multiple stakeholders, such as employees and customers. A top-down approach refers to leaders taking the responsibility to live and embed the values of the company.

One way to apply a bottom-up approach to establish new values for a company is to ask employees, customers, and shareholders to complete two surveys. The first survey measures how relevant stakeholders (employees, customers, and shareholders) perceive (a) their own values, (b) the current values in the organization, and (c) the values required to achieve the higher-purpose vision. The results of this survey could then be consolidated to reveal the link between stakeholder values, current company values, and desired company values. The consolidated survey results are then used to identify a potential list of values for the organization.

Thereafter, a second survey can be sent to employees, customers, and shareholders, in which they (a) rank the list of potential values in terms of importance to achieve the higher-purpose vision of the company and (b) describe behavioral indicators for each value. The ranking results of the second survey can then be used to finalize a list of values for the company, and the qualitative descriptions of the values can be used to establish behavioral indicators for each value.

Once the Organizational Values Framework has been finalized, leaders must take responsibility for implementing and embedding the values in the company.

8.2.1.3 Establish an organizational creed

The **third objective** of the *Preparation* phase is to develop an organizational creed. An organizational creed describes (a) the reason why an organization exists, (b) the aim of the organization, and the (c) way employees should behave. An organizational creed is thus the consolidation of the higher-purpose vision and the Organizational Values Framework.

An organizational creed can be created by conducting several workshops with the leadership teams of the organization. During these workshops, each leadership team uses the higher-purpose vision and Organizational Values Framework to propose an organizational creed. All proposals can then be consolidated by an external consultant to finalize an organizational creed for the company.

8.2.2 Phase 2: Implementation

This phase consists of seven stages to implement servant leadership in an organization, namely (1) evaluate leadership values and intent, (2) align leadership values and intent, (3) translate and execute a higher-purpose vision, (4) become a role model and ambassador, (5) align, care for, and grow employees, (6) continuously monitor and improve, and (7) apply the Talent Wheel of Servant Leadership.

8.2.2.1 Stage 1: Evaluate leadership values and intent

The *Implementation* phase starts with the evaluation and alignment of leadership values and intentions. Several psychometric and other assessments can be used in this process, such as a Personal Values Assessment and a Heartstyle Assessment. The results of these assessments can then be used to compare the values of leaders with the Organizational Values Framework.

8.2.2.2 Stage 2: Align leadership values and intent

The second stage of the *Implementation* phase is to align the current leadership behavior of an individual with the desired leadership behavior and Organizational Values Framework. Leadership coaching can be used to achieve this. For example, a professional coach could use the Personal

Values and Heartstyle assessment results of an individual to coach the leader to adopt more effective leadership behavior, in line with the Organizational Values Framework. The Thought Process Map (discussed in Chapter 4) can also be used in these coaching sessions. Once the personal values and intent of leaders have been evaluated and aligned, the five phases of the Systematic Servant Leadership Model can be implemented.

8.2.2.3 Stage 3: Translate and execute the higher-purpose vision

The third stage in the *Implementation* phase is to translate and execute the higher purpose of the organization by applying the soldier-leadership function. The **first objective** in this stage is to translate the higher-purpose vision into a mission, strategy, and positional goals. This can be done by conducting management, departmental, and work-unit workshops in which the department or work unit establishes a departmental or work-unit strategy that supports the higher-purpose vision of the organization. Once a strategy has been established, specific positional and employee goals must be set. The Strategic Alignment Matrix (discussed in Chapter 3) can be used in the workshop, to align the strategy and employee goals with the higher-purpose vision of the company. These Departmental and work-unit strategies should be reviewed and authorized by senior and executive management.

The **second objective** of Stage 3 of the *Implementation* phase is to develop and align business processes, systems, and policies to support the higher-purpose vision, mission, and strategy of the company. This can be done by means of management workshops, systems analysis workshops, and policy and procedure workshops. Management workshops would focus on developing specific business processes for each function or value chain in the organization, and systems analysis workshops would determine or analyze the systems required to mobilize the business processes of the organization. During policy and procedure workshops, specific policies and procedures are developed and formalized in line with the higher-purpose vision and Organizational Values Framework. These business processes, systems, and policies should be implemented after development, using effective change management processes.

The **third objective** of this stage is to develop Capability and Capacity

Frameworks that will support the higher-purpose vision, mission, and strategy of the company. This can be done by means of management workshops to establish a Responsibility Matrix for each function or value chain in the organization. A Responsibility Matrix lists (a) the type of positions required in each function or value chain, (b) the responsibilities and duties of each position according to the relevant business processes, and (c) the knowledge, skills, and attribute requirements for each position. The information of the Responsibility Matrix is then used to compile a Job Profile for each position in the organization.

8.2.2.4 Stage 4: Leaders become role models and ambassadors

This stage of the *Implementation* phase is where leaders become role models for employees, as well as ambassadors of the higher-purpose vision of the organization, by applying the athlete-leadership function. The **first objective** in this stage is leaders becoming aware of their strengths and development areas. Psychometric assessments can be used to identify a leader's cognitive ability, emotional intelligence, and personal attributes, and a 360-degree survey can be used to evaluate a leader's behavior from the perspective of others (colleagues, superiors, direct reports, and customers). After assessment, feedback and coaching sessions should be scheduled with each leader, to (a) provide constructive feedback regarding the assessment results and (b) to give him or her an opportunity to identify any personal strengths and development areas and to (c) list and implement personal development actions.

The **second objective** of Stage 4 of the *Implementation* phase is enhanced personal and leadership effectiveness of leaders. A Personal Development Plan should be compiled for each leader, which should list personal development requirements, activities, and timelines. The activities should include fundamental, experiential, and personal transformation learning activities. Progress of the leader must be tracked, and leaders must practice regular personal reflection as part of their personal development. The Reflection Guide provided in Chapter 4 could be useful in this regard. Some form of incentive may be offered to leaders once they have completed all the required development, coaching, and reflection activities per their

Personal Development Plan. In this way, personal development and, ultimately, servant leadership are recognized and rewarded.

8.2.2.5 Stage 5: Align, care for, and grow employees

This stage in the *Implementation* phase entails aligning, caring for, and growing employees by applying the farmer-leadership function. The **first objective** of this stage is to align the life purpose, knowledge, skills, and natural talent of employees to a specific position, in line with the higher-purpose vision of the organization. The department responsible for organizational development or people management should design effective recruitment and selection policies, procedures, systems, and application toolkits to equip leaders with the systems and resources to align employees effectively. Some of the application resources that should be developed for leaders is CV Screening Scorecards or systems and Competency-based Interview Guides. CV Screening Scorecards are useful in shortlisting applications, and a Competency-based Interview Guide is a useful tool with which to evaluate individuals objectively during the interview process. Leaders must be trained on the application of recruitment and selection policies, procedures, systems, and resources. Such training will enable them to effectively align employees to positions that support the execution of the higher-purpose vision of the company.

Psychometric assessments are valuable in the alignment process. The required skills and attributes of the position and the Organizational Values Framework can be used to establish psychometric assessment benchmarks for each position listed in the Capacity Framework of the organization. The psychometric assessment results of an applicant can then be compared with the psychometric benchmarks of the relevant position, to determine the best person–job fit. Psychometric assessments should never be used in isolation to make final decisions; a selection committee must rather use a combination of sources of information, such as CV Screening Scorecards, Competency-based Interview Guides, and psychometric assessments, to select the best candidate for the position.

The **second objective** of Stage 5 of the *Implementation* phase is to care for employees, which refers to creating a conducive work climate and a culture in which employees flourish. Organizational Diagnostic

Surveys are valuable tools to measure employee work engagement levels and to determine the drivers and outcomes of work engagement in the organization. An Organizational Climate and Culture Diagnostic Survey must measure (a) the drivers of work engagement in the organization — job demands and job resources, (b) the work engagement levels of employees, (c) the limitations to work engagement, such as employee burnout and ill health, and (d) the outcomes of work engagement, such as employee retention, corporate citizenship behavior, and productivity. The results of the Organizational Diagnostic Survey will provide leaders with adequate information to (a) evaluate the current levels of employee work engagement in the organization, (b) understand how work engagement is impacting employees' and the organization's performance, and (c) to determine how to enhance work engagement in the organization.

Organizational diagnostic results should be filtered by division, department, and work unit, and constructive feedback must be provided to the leaders of these areas after assessment. In this way, each leader will receive relevant information on how to improve the work climate and culture in his or her division, department, or work unit. Management workshops might be an effective way to communicate organizational diagnostic results. The objectives of these management workshops are to (a) discuss organizational diagnostic results, (b) identify specific and holistic organizational development areas, and to (c) plan interventions to improve the work climate and culture of the organization.

Management workshops must be conducted per division, department, or work unit, as their results and development areas may differ, and holistic and tailored strategies must then be developed and implemented in each area. A follow-up Diagnostic Survey should be conducted after the interventions have been implemented, to determine whether the interventions were successful in enhancing the work engagement of employees.

The **third objective** of Stage 5 of the *Implementation* phase is to grow and empower employees. To achieve this objective, the department responsible for organizational development, learning and development, or people management must develop learning and development policies, procedures, systems, and resources to enable leaders to continuously grow and empower employees, in line with the Capability Framework of the company, to support the higher-purpose vision of the organization.

Learning and development systems and resources should include a Career Plan and a Personal Development Plan for each employee in the organization, and leaders must be trained on their application.

After training, leaders must compile a Career Plan and a Personal Development Plan for the employees in their respective divisions, departments, or work units. The Career Plan template and the Personal Development Plan template provided in Chapter 6 could be used in this process. Leaders must monitor individual progress on these plans, and they should grow their employees by means of coaching and mentoring. In this way, leaders are actively involved in the growth and empowerment of employees to enable them to achieve the higher-purpose vision of the company.

8.2.2.6 Stage 6: Continuously monitor and improve

The sixth stage in the *Implementation* phase is to continuously monitor and improve by applying the steward-leadership function. The **first objective** in this stage is to monitor performance continuously. The organizational development department in the company should facilitate the development of the performance management policy, procedure, system, and application toolkits to equip leaders with the necessary resources to monitor performance adequately and consistently. The performance management system should enable a leader to (a) set stewardship plans (performance targets) for employees, in line with vision, mission and strategy of the company, as well as with the goals of the position (per the translation process during Stage 2 of the *Implementation* phase), (b) monitor and record employee performance and work-unit performance, and (c) conduct formal performance reviews. A performance management system should thus track the progress made towards achieving the higher-purpose vision, mission, and strategy of the organization, and should indicate performance strengths and gaps per division, department, work unit, and employee.

Once the performance management system and policies, procedures, and application resources have been developed, leaders should be trained to use these effectively, and then implement them in their respective areas. Implementation is considered successful when (a) each employee in the organization has a Stewardship Plan (performance targets) that supports the higher-purpose vision, mission, and strategy of the organization, (b) employee, work-unit, departmental, and divisional performance is regularly reviewed and recorded, and (c) employee and organizational performance achievements are rewarded and gaps are identified and addressed.

The Strategic Alignment Matrix (discussed in Chapter 3) and the Stewardship Plan templates (provided in Chapter 5) might be useful to monitor performance. In Stage 2 of the *Implementation* phase, the Strategic Alignment Matrix was used to translate the higher-purpose vision into employee goals. These employee goals can be transferred to the Stewardship Plan, to indicate when the goals should be completed and how success will be measured. The Stewardship Plan should also indicate the performance review dates (*Omega* check-in dates), when both the employee and the leader will review progress towards achieving the goals.

The **second objective** of Stage 6 of the *Implementation* phase is to continuously improve the products, services, processes, policies, and systems of the organization. This can be done by scheduling regular improvement workshops to review a policy, process, system, product, or service and to establish an action plan to improve these. The action plan should then be implemented and the impact thereof measured in a next review session.

An entrepreneurial and innovation program is another way to stimulate continuous improvement in the organization. In such a program, the organization provides its employees, suppliers, customers, and members of society the opportunity to propose a new idea to either (a) improve a new product, service, system, process, or policy for the company, or (b) initiate new ones. The best proposal should be (a) rewarded by the company, (b) funded by the shareholders, and (c) implemented by the employees.

Improvement should always be done to the benefit of multiple stakeholders. The short- and long-term impact of any improvement must be predicted prior to implementation and be measured during implementation, to ensure all stakeholders benefit from the improvement. If the improvement only benefits one stakeholder, it should not be implemented, and another solution must be considered — one that creates value for multiple stakeholders (customers, employees, suppliers, shareholders, society, and the environment).

8.2.2.7 Stage 7: Apply the Talent Wheel of Servant Leadership

The seventh stage of the *Implementation* phase is to implement the Talent Wheel of Servant Leadership. In this phase, leaders activate the informal process to develop servant-leaders in their respective divisions, departments, and work units, as discussed in Chapter 7. The phases and activities of the Talent Wheel of Servant Leadership must be incorporated into the company's talent management policies, procedures, and systems. Application resources must also be designed, to enable leaders to apply the Talent Wheel of Servant Leadership. Leaders must then be trained to apply the talent management policy, processes, systems, and resources in the organization.

Leaders are furthermore responsible for helping employees complete all the developmental activities of the Talent Wheel of Servant Leadership and for providing regular coaching and mentoring. The overall implementation progress of this Talent Wheel of Servant Leadership should be monitored, and employee achievements must be archived on a talent management system. In this way, (a) the potential of employees can be recorded, (b) the readiness of employees can be tracked, and (c) overall implementation success can be measured. The main goal of this process is to identify and grow potential leaders in the organization who are readily available to take up leadership positions as the company grows.

8.2.3 Phases 3: Sustainability

The last phase in implementing servant leadership is to ensure its sustainability. In this phase, the various systems, platforms, and resources are developed or reviewed to embed the implementation of servant leadership in the organization. This phase requires five systems, namely (1) a recruitment and selection system, (2) a performance management system, (3) a learning and development system, (4) a job-profiling system, and (5) a talent management system. It also requires two platforms, namely (1) a communication platform and (2) a knowledge center, and two types of sustainability resources, namely (1) a Leadership Culture Diagnostic Survey and (2) business cases.

8.2.3.1 The recruitment and selection system

The first system to be embedded or reviewed is a recruitment and selection system. The primary objective of this system is to effectively align employees to positions per the Capacity and Capability Frameworks of the company. A recruitment and selection system should simplify the process of aligning employees to positions, and should include at least the following functionalities: (1) vacancy advertisement, (2) online application processing, (3) automatic CV-screening according to the knowledge, skills, and experience requirements of a position, (4) scoring of competency-based interviews, (5) recording of the results of psychometric assessments, (6) archiving reference-check information, and (7) a consolidated comparison report in which the information gathered through the other functionalities is summarized. A selection panel or leader can then use the system to make informed decisions on which applicant offers the best person–job fit and person–organization fit.

The data collected during the psychometric assessments in Stages 1 and 5 of the *Implementation* phase can be used to create psychometric assessment benchmarks in the company. For example, the Values and Heartstyle Assessments' data of top-performing servant-leaders (collected in Stage 1 of the *Implementation* phase) are valuable in creating psychometric assessment benchmarks for the company in recruiting and selecting leaders. The same can be done for the psychometric assessments conducted in Stage 5 of the *Implementation* phase. The data of top-performing employees per position can be used to create internal psychometric assessment benchmarks for each position and to recruit and select individuals. Psychometric assessment benchmarks should be incorporated into the recruitment and selection system. In this way, the psychometric assessment results of applicants can be compared with the internal psychometric assessment benchmarks of the company and used to select the best person for the job and the organization.

8.2.3.2 The performance management system

The second system to be established or reviewed is a performance management system. The purpose of this system is to (1) set performance targets, (2) monitor and track performance progress, and to (3) archive performance review records. During Stage 3 of the *Implementation* phase, the higher-purpose vision of the company was translated into company, divisional, departmental, and work unit strategies, as well as employee goals, using the Strategic Alignment Matrix (refer to Objective 1 of Stage 3 of the *Implementation* phase). A Stewardship Plan was also developed for each employee in Stage 6 of the *Implementation* phase (refer to Objective 1 of Stage 6 of the *Implementation* phase) in which specific measures of success, timelines, and review dates were allocated to each positional goal. This information should be incorporated into the performance management system and used to establish a Company Performance Scorecard and a Positional Performance Scorecard.

The Company Performance Scorecard lists the strategic objectives of the company, together with the measure of success and a target date for each goal, in line with the higher-purpose vision of the company. The Positional Performance Scorecard lists the positional goals that support the higher-purpose vision, mission, and strategy of the company, and include a measure of success and a timeline for each goal. The strategic and positional goals listed in the Strategic Alignment Matrix and finalized in the Stewardship Plans can thus be captured on the performance management system, to track, monitor, and review performance.

The Capability and Capacity Frameworks of the organization were established in Stage 3 of the *Implementation* phase, using a Responsibility Matrix to list the key responsibilities and performance areas of each position (refer to Objective 3 of Stage 3 of the *Implementation* phase). This information can be added to the Positional Performance Scorecard on the performance management system. Leaders can then use the performance management system to monitor, review, and record positional performance in line with the Capability and Capacity Frameworks.

The performance management system should, in addition, include a Behavioral Performance Scorecard. This is used to evaluate the desired leadership and employee behaviors, in accordance with the Organizational Values Framework, which was established during the *Preparation* phase. The Organizational Values Framework can be used in the *Sustainability* phase to develop a Behavioral Scorecard for the performance management system.

The information and data collected during the *Preparation* and *Implementation* phases are not only used to establish Behavioral, Company, and Positional Scorecards, but can also be used to evaluate performance. For example, the data collected during Stage 2 of the *Implementation* phase (refer to Objective 1 of Stage 2 of the *Implementation* phase) can be used to evaluate the performance of leaders on the Behavioral Scorecard of the performance management system. In Stage 2 of the *Implementation* phase, the values and intent of leaders were also aligned to the Organizational Values Framework and higher-purpose vision of the organization. The progress and performance of a leader during this phase can therefore be reviewed using the Behavioral Scorecard of the performance management system.

Once Behavioral, Company, and Positional Scorecards have been incorporated into the performance management system, leaders can use the system to track, monitor, and review performance in line with the higher-purpose vision, mission, and strategy of the organization. The performance reviews during Stage 6 of the *Implementation* phase (refer to Objective 1 of Stage 6) are a continuous activity and should be captured on the performance management system, to build a database of performance records per employee, work unit, department, and division, and for the organization. In this way, performance towards achieving the higher-purpose vision can be monitored and performance gaps can be identified and addressed.

8.2.3.3 The learning and development system

Servant-leadership competencies should also be incorporated into the learning and development system of the company. The main purpose of a learning and development system is to coordinate, monitor, and record learning and development activities in the company. The primary functions of a learning and development system should be to (a) schedule learning activities, (b) list competency gaps per employee, (c) establish Personal Development Plans, (d) monitor and track the progress on Personal Development Plans per employee, (e) archive learning and development information, and (f) to report learning and development activities and progress. A learning and development system could furthermore include competency-based courses according to the Capability Framework and Job Profiles. In this way, competency gaps can be closed with specific courses.

The information captured in the Personal Development Plans of leaders in Stage 4 of the *Implementation* phase (refer to Objective 2 of Stage 4 of the *Implementation* phase) must also be captured on the learning and development system, to track progress automatically. As the leader completes the activities in his or her Personal Development Plan, the department responsible for learning and development should update the system accordingly.

During Stage 5 of the *Implementation* phase, the leader drafted Personal Development Plans for employees in his or her division, department, or work unit (refer to Objective 3 of Stage 5 of the *Implementation* phase). This information could be captured on the learning and development system, so that leaders can track employees' progress. The department responsible for learning and development must update the system as employees complete learning and development activities, and update Personal Development Plans accordingly. Leaders can then retrieve development progress reports from the system.

8.2.3.4 Job profiling system

Another system that should be embedded or updated in the organization after the *Implementation* phase is a job profiling system. The purpose of a job profiling system is to (a) list the job titles and job families per the Capacity Framework of the organization, (b) indicate the required competencies per position, per the Capability Framework, and to (c) compile the Job Profile for each position, per the Capability and Capacity Frameworks of the company, to achieve the higher-purpose vision of the company.

During Stage 3 of the *Implementation* phase (refer to Objective 3 of Stage 3 of the *Implementation* phase), leaders translated the higher-purpose vision, mission, and strategy into Capability and Capacity Frameworks for the company, and established a Responsibility Matrix for each function, listing the required positions, responsibilities, and competencies to achieve the higher-purpose vision. The information contained in the Responsibility Matrix can be used to (a) list and categorize job titles, (b) establish a Competency Framework for the company, and (c) compile a Job Profile for each position. This information must be captured on a job profiling system. The Job Profiles can then be used in recruitment and selection, learning and development, and in talent management processes (for selection, training, and promotion).

8.2.3.5 *Talent management system*

The fifth system to be embedded after the *Implementation* phase is a talent management system. The general aim of this system is to automate, track, and report all talent-related activities in the organization. The specific objectives of a talent management system are to (a) identify potential servant-leaders, (b) monitor and track the development of potential servant-leaders, and (c) determine the readiness of a potential servant-leader for a future leadership position. A talent management system should thus include the following functionalities: (a) talent identification, (b) talent development, (c) talent monitoring, and (d) talent deployment.

A talent management system should, firstly, identify potential servant-leaders in the organization by comparing the knowledge, skills, values, talents, and life purpose of an employee with the requirements of a leadership position. The system can then be used to identify potential successors.

Secondly, a talent management system should track the development of potential servant-leaders in the organization. During Stage 7 of the *Implementation* phase, leaders implemented the Talent Wheel of Servant Leadership to transform employees into servant-leaders (refer to Objective 1 of Stage 7 of the *Implementation* phase). The development activities of the Talent Wheel of Servant Leadership (as well as those of the Framework for Effective Servant-leadership Development) should be incorporated into the talent management system, allowing leaders to track employee development during these processes. Individual, team, and organizational reports can then be extracted from the system to determine the progress of talent development in the company. Leaders can use these progress reports to identify talent gaps in the organization and to implement interventions to close development gaps.

The talent management system should, thirdly, monitor talent in the organization. Once the development activities of the Talent Wheel of Servant Leadership and the Framework for Effective Servant-leadership Development have been captured on the talent management system, leaders could use the system to monitor the development of servant-leaders in the company and to track talent readiness in the organization. In other words, leaders could use the system to determine when potential servant-leaders will become ready to fill future leadership positions. The system could also flag talent risks when a scarcity of talent is evident in the organization. Proactive development efforts could then be implemented to ensure talent is readily available as the organization grows.

Fourth, a talent management system should simplify the deployment of talent. When new leadership positions become available in the organization, the talent management system should indicate which talent in the organization is ready to fill the positions. The development progress of potential servant-leaders should therefore be updated on the talent management system when they complete the development activities of the Talent Wheel of Servant Leadership (per Objective 1 of Stage 7 of the *Implementation* phase), as well as the development activities of the Framework for Effective Servant-leadership Development (discussed in Chapter 7). The talent management system can then identify when an employee will be ready to take up a new leadership position.

Leaders could furthermore use the talent management system to establish a succession plan for each division, department, and work unit. The information gathered in Stage 7 of the *Implementation* phase could be used to identify possible successors for leadership positions. Personal Development Plans could then be established for those employees, to prepare them for a future leadership position. The development progress of successors should be tracked on the system, to establish when employees are ready for promotion.

8.2.3.6 Communication platform

The first platform that should be embedded within the organization after the *Implementation* phase of servant leadership is an internal communication platform. An internal communication platform is used to communicate relevant and important information to employees on a regular basis. This platform could consist of different communication mediums, such as social media, newsletters, emails, videos, posters, marketing campaigns, and staff meetings.

The main purpose of the communication platform should be to activate and encourage employees to practice servant leadership after the initial implementation thereof in the organization. A communication platform should communicate (a) the importance of servant leadership, (b) the definition, (c) practices, (d) and results of servant leadership, as well as (e) new research in the field. In this way, the communication platform will (a) remind employees why servant leadership is the preferred leadership practice in the organization, (b) describe how employees could practice servant leadership in the organization, and (c) announce the benefits and impact of servant leadership in the current context.

A formal marketing campaign could create awareness around the reasons for and the application and the benefits of servant leadership, especially in the early stages after implementation. Such a marketing campaign must (a) have a clear purpose, (b) follow a structured communication plan, (c) use various mediums, and (d) engage and activate the target audience.

Once the purpose of the marketing campaign has been established, a formal and structured Communication Plan should be drafted and implemented, in line with the main objective of the marking campaign. A Communication Plan consists of the mediums, messages, and time frames of communication. In other words, it lists and describes (a) the messages that will be communicated to employees to practice servant leadership, (b) the mediums that will be used to communicate the messages, and (c) the time frames for communication.

After a Communication Plan has been drafted, it should be implemented via the various communication mediums. A variety of communication mediums will widen the impact of communication and ensure that the same messages are repeated in different ways and formats. For example, to communicate the practice of servant leadership (a) an article can be published in a corporate newsletter, (b) a video of the CEO explaining the principles and practices of servant leadership can be sent via email, (c) a divisional leader can share a real-life business case during a staff conference, and (d) new research by an external expert could be published on the corporate social media instrument.

The success of a marketing campaign should be measured by the increase in servant-leadership behavior in the organization. Employee and leadership evaluation surveys to collect and compare data might be useful in this regard.

8.2.3.7 Knowledge center

The second platform to be embedded within the company after the *Implementation* phase of servant leadership is a knowledge center. This is an online platform where employees who completed a servant-leadership development program can access additional information on the topic. A knowledge center consists of articles, videos, podcasts, application toolkits, and other related resources on servant leadership. Employees who completed a servant-leadership development program can then access the information on the knowledge center at any time, and the knowledge center could also send employees regular knowledge feeds via email, sms, or social media, with links to articles, videos, podcasts, and application toolkits.

A knowledge center should also provide an opportunity for employees to share experiential insights via discussion forums or blogs. Once employees have completed a servant-leadership development program, they should share their experiential insights on the implementation and benefits of servant leadership on the knowledge center by either writing an article, publishing a business case, sharing a story via a video recording, engaging in a group discussion, or writing a blog. In this way, employees can learn from each other why servant leadership is important, how servant leadership can be implemented, and what the benefits of servant leadership are.

It is important to keep a knowledge center up to date with new information and resources on servant leadership and to maintain the momentum of the implementation of servant leadership using the latest information. A dedicated person or team should be appointed to manage this platform and enroll new employees on the platform.

One way to update a knowledge center is to invite external experts on servant leadership to (a) present video-recorded masterclasses in the organization on servant leadership, (b) write an article on new research in the field of servant leadership, (c) facilitate webinars related to servant leadership, and to (d) initiate group discussions on servant leadership via the knowledge center. These videos, articles, webinars, and group discussions can then be published in the knowledge center and sent to employees who have completed the program.

8.2.3.8 Leadership Culture Diagnostic Survey

The first type of resource to be embedded within the organization after the *Implementation* phase of servant leadership is a Leadership Culture Diagnostic Survey. This is a 360-degree survey in which employees evaluate the leadership culture and behavior in the organization. This survey should measure the (a) heart type of leaders, (b) behavior of leaders, as well as the (c) competence level of leaders from the perspective of direct reports, colleagues, superiors, and even customers. The Survey must therefore measure servant-leadership intent (loving leadership heart), servant-leadership characteristics (courage, altruism, authenticity, humility, integrity, listening, compassion, and accountability), and servant-leadership competencies (setting a compelling vision, personal capability, able to build relationships, empowerment, and stewardship).

Employees should complete the survey regularly, and the overall results should be filtered per division, department, and work unit, in order to track the servant-leadership behavior of each and make comparisons over time. The assessment data can also be used to identify and address development areas in the application of servant leadership per division, department, or work unit.

The first set of data on servant-leadership behavior and competence was collected during Stage 4 of the *Implementation* phase (refer to Objective 1 of Stage 4 of the *Implementation* phase). This data can be used as an interim benchmark of servant-leadership behavior in the company. Follow-up assessments should be compared with the benchmark scores of each division, department, or work unit, to determine any shifts in servant-leadership behavior and competence in the organization.

The assessment results of the Leadership Culture Diagnostic Survey can also be used to reward servant-leadership behavior and to identify and remedy poor or ineffective leadership behavior.

8.2.3.9 Business cases

The second type of resource to be embedded within the organization after the *Implementation* phase of servant leadership is the publication of business cases that show the impact of servant leadership.

During Stage 5 of the *Implementation* phase (refer to Objective 2 of Stage 5 of the *Implementation* phase), leaders initiated organizational development projects to improve the work climate and culture in their respective divisions, departments, and work units. The outcomes of these projects could be published as business cases.

During Stage 6 of the *Implementation* phase (refer to Objective 2 of Stage 6 of the *Implementation* phase), leaders developed action plans to improve the policies, procedures, systems, products, or services in their respective divisions, departments, or work units. The outcome and impact of these action plans could also be used as business cases. Through publication, leaders and employees can learn from each other regarding effective ways to apply servant-leadership principles and practices in the organization.

Business progress reports are also useful to show the effective implementation of servant leadership in the company. Divisional, departmental, and work-unit leaders should compile monthly or quarterly progress reports on the implementation of servant leadership in the organization. Business progress reports must be standardized according the standard implementation procedure of servant leadership, to track the status of implementation in each division, department or work unit. Inefficiencies can then be identified and proactively addressed.

The best business cases or progress reports should be recognized and rewarded by the company. For example, employees could vote each year for the best business cases in terms of impact in the organization, and the company can then reward those leaders. The leaders who made the most progress in the effective implementation of servant leadership could also be rewarded.

8.3 Interdependence of sustainability systems, platforms, and resources

The systems, platforms, and resources in the *Sustainability* phase are interdependent. For example, the Job Profiles are used, firstly, in the recruitment and selection system to develop CV Screening Scorecards, Competency-based Interview Guides, and psychometric assessment benchmarks per position. Secondly, the Job Profiles could be used to compile a Positional Scorecard in the performance management system for each position in the organization. Thirdly, the Job Profiles of the job profiling system could be used in the learning and development system, to establish competency-based courses per position, according to the positional competencies listed in each Job Profile. A fourth application of the Job Profile is to use it in the talent management system to select successors for future positions. The talent management system then compares the knowledge, skills, and experience of employees with the Job Profile of a future position, to determine the potential person–job fit.

Another example of the interdependence of sustainability systems, platforms, and resources is that the data of the Leadership Diagnostic Surveys can be used in the performance management system to evaluate the behavioral performance of leaders. The data of the Leadership Culture Diagnostic Surveys, progress reports, and published business cases can also be used to identify the top-performing leaders in the company. These leaders can then be rewarded as part of a marketing campaign published on the communication platform. Such a marketing campaign could include an awards ceremony where the best servant-leaders are recognized. Business cases and progress reports can also be used to update the knowledge center of the company and to initiate experiential discussions in the knowledge center. In this way, leaders can learn from each other how to implement servant leadership effectively in the company.

8.4 Conclusion

Chapter 1 of this book highlighted the destructive outcomes of self-serving leadership, such as fraud and corruption, stress-related ill health, poverty, economic problems, political instability, manipulation of capitalism, and low employee engagement levels. These destructive outcomes, evident in people, business, and society, indicate a need for a more effective leadership approach, such as servant leadership.

In Chapter 2, the main differentiating characteristics of a self-serving leader and a servant-leader were discussed in terms of the heart and intent of the leader. Three leader-heart types were described: a (1) prideful heart,

(2) a fearful heart, and (3) a loving heart. Chapter 2 also revealed that self-serving leaders lead from a prideful or fearful heart, whereas servant-leaders lead from a loving heart. The importance of personal and organizational values was also emphasized in Chapter 2.

The four functions of a servant-leader were discussed in Chapters 3, 4, 5, and 6, namely the (1) soldier-leadership function, (2) athlete-leadership function, (3) steward-leadership function, and the (4) farmer-leadership function. These chapters focused on the application of servant leadership through practical guidelines and objectives. The associated servant-leadership characteristics and competencies of each function were also discussed.

In Chapter 7, the four functions were summarized into two frameworks to develop servant-leaders, namely the (1) Talent Wheel of Servant Leadership and (2) the Framework for Effective Servant-leadership Development. The Talent Wheel of Servant Leadership proposes an informal process to transform employees into servant-leaders, and the Framework for Effective Servant-leadership Development proposes a formal process to develop servant leaders in an organization. Learning and development practitioners and leaders could use these two frameworks to cultivate servant-leaders in organizations.

In Chapter 8, the functions of a servant-leader and the Talent Wheel of Servant Leadership were consolidated into the Systematic Servant Leadership Model, and the process to apply this model in an organization was explained. Chapter 8 also provided a standard implementation procedure to apply servant leadership in organizations, which consists of three phases, namely (1) preparation, (2) implementation, and (3) sustainability. Organizational development practitioners, people management practitioners, and organizational leaders could use this procedure to implement servant leadership and cultivate a servant-leadership culture in an organization. In return, organizations will experience the benefits of servant leadership described in Chapter 1.

Reference list

Anderson, D., & Jahng, N. (2014). *Academic overview of the heartstyles indicator*. Retrieved from http://www.heartstyles.com/what-is-heartstyles

Bakker, A. B., & Demerouti, E. (2007). The job demands-resources model: State of the art. *Journal of Managerial Psychology, 22*(3), 309–328. doi:10.1108/02683940710733115

Bakker, A. B., & Demerouti, E. (2008). Towards a model of work engagement. *Career Development International, 13*(3), 209–223. doi:10.1108/13620430810870476

Barret, R. (2006). *Building a values-driven organization: A whole system approach to cultural transformation*. Burlington: Elsevier.

Blanchard, K. (2010). *Leading at a higher level: Blanchard on leadership and creating high performing organizations*. New Jersey: FT Press.

Blanchard, K., Zigarmi, P., Zigarmi, D., & Halsey, V. (2013). *Situational leadership II*. San Diego, CA: Ken Blanchard Companies.

Coetzer, M. F. (2018a). A conceptual framework to operationalise servant leadership within an organisation. In D. van Dierendonck & K. Patterson (Eds.), *Practising servant leadership: Developments in implementation*. London: Palgrave Macmillian.

Coetzer, M. F. (2018b). *The impact of a servant leadership intervention on work engagement and burnout* (Doctoral Thesis). University of Johannesburg.

Coetzer, M. F., Bussin, M., & Geldenhuys, M. (2017). The functions of a servant leader. *Administrative Sciences, 7*(5), 1–32. doi:10.3390/admsci7010005

De Braine, R., & Roodt, G. (2011). The Job Demands–Resources Model as predictor of work identity and work engagement: A comparative analysis. *SA Journal of Industrial Psychology, 37*(2), 1–11. doi:10.4102/sajip.v37i2.889

De Waal, A. (2012). Characteristics of high performance organisations. *Journal of Management Research, 4*(4), 39–71. doi:10.5296/jmr.v4i4.2062

Frey, C. B., & Osborne, M. A. (2017). The future of employment: How susceptible are jobs to computerisation? *Technological Forecasting and Social Change, 114*, 254–280. doi:10.1016/j.techfore.2016.08.019

Gallup. (2013). *State of the global workplace: Employee engagement insights for business leaders worldwide.* Retrieved from http://www.gallup.com/strategicconsulting/164735/state-global-workplace.aspx

Goleman, D. (2004). What makes a leader? Retrieved from https://hbr.org/2004/01/what-makes-a-leader

Greenleaf, R. K. (1998). *The power of servant-leadership.* San Francisco, CA: Berrett-Koehler Publishers.

Gunter, M. H. (2013). *Brain-based coaching: Participant manual 8.0.* Australia: Neuroleadership Group.

Hedges, C. (2003). What every person should know about war. Retrieved from http://www.nytimes.com/2003/07/06/books/chapters/0713-1st-hedges.html?pagewanted=all

International Labour Organization and Walk Free Foundation. (2017). *Global estimates of modern slavery.* Retrieved from http://www.ilo.org/global/publications/books/WCMS_575479/lang--en/index.htm

Kaplan, R. S., & Norton, D. P. (1992). The balanced scorecard: Measures that drive performance. *Harvard Business Review, 72*(1), 71–79. Retrieved from https://pdfs.semanticscholar.org/dcca/93c621f618e511a94e15384e52ff893be3c7.pdf

Lakner, C., Azevedo, J. P., Mahler, D., & Prydz, E. B. (2018). April 2018 global poverty update from the World Bank. Retrieved from http://blogs.worldbank.org/developmenttalk/april-2018-global-poverty-update-world-bank

Leaf, C. (2013). *Switch on your brain: The key to peak happiness, thinking, and health.* Grand Rapids, MI: Baker Publishing Group.

Lombardo, M. M., & Eichinger, R. W. (2006). *The career architect development planner* (4th ed.). Minneapolis, MN: Lominger Limited Inc.

Mackey, J., & Sisodia, R. (2014). *Conscious capitalism: Liberating the heroic spirit of business*. New York: Harvard Business School Publishing Corporation.

Nagtzaam, G. (2009). Environmental exploitation: An analysis and taxonomy. In L. Leonard & J. Barry (Eds.), *The transition to sustainable living and practice: Advances in ecopolitics* (pp. 101–116). Emerald Group Publishing Limited.

Owen, K., Mundy, R., Guild, W., & Guild, R. (2001). Creating and sustaining the high performance organization. *Managing Service Quality: An International Journal, 11*(1), 10–21. doi:10.1108/09604520110362443

PricewaterhouseCoopers. (2018). *The dawn of proactivity: Countering threats from inside and out*. Retrieved from https://www.pwc.co.za/en/assets/pdf/gecs-2018.pdf

Prinsloo, M., & Prinsloo, R. (2012). *Cognitive process profile*. London: Cognadev UK Ltd.

Rothmann, I. (2008). *South African Employee Health and Wellness Survey: User manual*. Potchefstroom, South Africa: Afriforte.

Schaufeli, W. B. (2003). Past performance and future perspectives of burnout research. *SA Journal of Industrial Psychology, 29*(4), 1–15. doi:10.4102/sajip.v29i4.127

Schaufeli, W. B. (2015). Engaging leadership in the job demands-resources model. *Career Development International, 20*(5), 446–463. doi:10.1108/02683940010305270

Schaufeli, W. B., & Bakker, A. B. (2004). Job demands, job resources, and their relationship with burnout and engagement: A multi-sample study. *Journal of Organizational Behavior, 25*(3), 293–315. doi:10.1002/job.248

Schaufeli, W. B., Bakker, A. B., & Salanova, M. (2006). The measurement of work engagement with a short questionnaire: A cross-national study. *Educational and Psychological Measurement, 66*(4), 701–716. doi:10.1177/0013164405282471

Sisodia, R., Sheth, J., & Wolfe, D. (2014). *Firms of endearment: How world-class companies profit from passion and purpose*. New Jersey: Pearson Education.

Stein, S. J., & Book, H. E. (2011). *The EQ edge: Emotional intelligence and your success* (3rd ed.). Mississauga, Canada: Jossey-Bass.

United Nations. (2018). *World economic situation and prospects 2018*. Retrieved from https://www.un.org/development/desa/dpad/wp-content/uploads/sites/45/publication/WESP2018_Full_Web-1.pdf

Viljoen, H., & De Kock, F. (2012). *Human capital return-on-investment (HCROI) in South African companies listed on the Johannesburg Stock Exchange (JSE)* (Master's Thesis). University of Stellenbosch.

World Economic Forum. (2016). *The future of jobs: Employment, skills and workforce strategy for the fourth industrial revolution*. Retrieved from http://www3.weforum.org/docs/WEF_Future_of_Jobs.pdf

World Health Organization. (2015). *Assessing national capacity for the prevention and control of noncommunicable diseases*. Retrieved from http://www.who.int/ncds/surveillance/ncd-capacity/en/

Zweynert, A. (2015). What is modern slavery? Retrieved from http://www.weforum.org/2015/12/what-is-modern-slavery/

Appendix A

APPLICATION TOOLS AND TEMPLATES

Strategic Alignment Matrix (template)

HIGHER-PURPOSE VISION

Our vision is...

MISSION

Our mission is...

STRATEGIC AIM 1
Objective 1

STRATEGIC AIM 2
Objective 2

STRATEGIC AIM 3
Objective 2

DEPARTMENT / WORK-UNIT AIM

Strategic aim	Measure of success	Target date
Objective 1.1	Measure 1.1	Date 1.1
Objective 1.2	Measure 1.2	Date 1.2
Objective 1.3	Measure 1.3	Date 1.3
Objective 1.4	Measure 1.4	Date 1.4

DEPARTMENT / WORK-UNIT AIM

Strategic aim	Measure of success	Target date
Objective 2.1	Measure 2.1	Date 2.1
Objective 2.2	Measure 2.2	Date 2.2
Objective 2.3	Measure 2.3	Date 2.3
Objective 2.4	Measure 2.4	Date 2.4

DEPARTMENT / WORK-UNIT AIM

Strategic aim	Measure of success	Target date
Objective 3.1	Measure 3.1	Date 3.1
Objective 3.2	Measure 3.2	Date 3.2
Objective 3.3	Measure 3.3	Date 3.3
Objective 3.4	Measure 3.4	Date 3.4

Objective 1.1

EMPLOYEE GOALS

Employee name	Goal	Measure of success	Target date

Objective 1.2

EMPLOYEE GOALS

Employee name	Goal	Measure of success	Target date

Objective 2.1

EMPLOYEE GOALS

Employee name	Goal	Measure of success	Target date

Objective 2.2

EMPLOYEE GOALS

Employee name	Goal	Measure of success	Target date

Objective 3.1

EMPLOYEE GOALS

Employee name	Goal	Measure of success	Target date

Objective 3.2

EMPLOYEE GOALS

Employee name	Goal	Measure of success	Target date

Objective 1.3

EMPLOYEE GOALS

Employee name	Goal	Measure of success	Target date

Objective 2.3

EMPLOYEE GOALS

Employee name	Goal	Measure of success	Target date

Objective 3.3

EMPLOYEE GOALS

Employee name	Goal	Measure of success	Target date

Objective 1.4

EMPLOYEE GOALS

Employee name	Goal	Measure of success	Target date

Objective 2.4

EMPLOYEE GOALS

Employee name	Goal	Measure of success	Target date

Objective 3.4

EMPLOYEE GOALS

Employee name	Goal	Measure of success	Target date

INDIVIDUAL PASSION AND PURPOSE GUIDE

Individual passion statement:
Answer the following questions honestly.

1. Imagine you had no limitations or barriers in terms of money, ability, time, or circumstances. What type of work would you do voluntarily?

2. Which task, job, or activity did you enjoy most so far in your career?

3. If anything is possible, what would you stop doing today and start doing tomorrow?

4. Review your answers in the previous questions and write an individual passion statement.

    I am passionate about ...

Individual purpose statement:

Answer the following questions honestly.

1. In your view, what unique contribution should you make to this world?

2. Why would the world be worse off without you in it?

3. What positive impact (or legacy) should you make to this world before leaving it?

4. Why do people, organizations, and the society need you?

5. What would you consider to be your main skills or competencies?

6. What type of expert knowledge do you possess?

7. What can you do with ease that others seem to struggle with (natural talents)?

8. What do you consider to be your personality strengths?

9. List 3 to 5 values you would like to live by (that would determine your behavior, judgement, and focus in life).

10. Reflect on your answers above and write a life purpose statement.

My purpose in life is to… (What), because… (Why). I will achieve this purpose by applying my knowledge of…, my skills of…, my natural talent(s) of…, and my attributes of… (How).

The values I live by are…

THOUGH PROCESS MAP

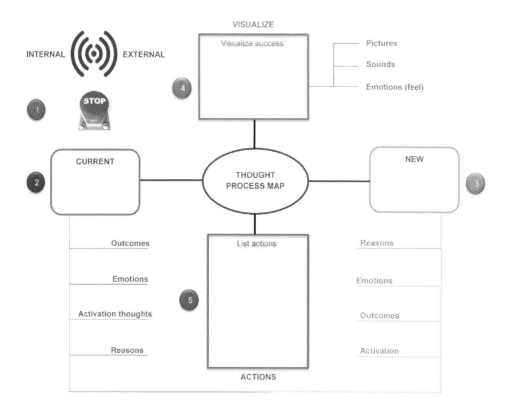

INTERNAL   EXTERNAL

VISUALIZE

Visualize success:

Pictures

Sounds

Emotions (feel)

1

STOP

4

CURRENT

THOUGHT
PROCESS MAP

NEW

2

3

Outcomes

Emotions

Activation thoughts

Reasons

List actions

5

Reasons

Emotions

Outcomes

Activation

ACTIONS

Step 1: STOP and THINK

When a certain stimulus activates an ineffective behavior, stop and think. Think about the impact of the current ineffective behavior (per Step 2, below) and think about the benefits of a new more effective behavior (per Steps 3 and 4, below).

Step 2: Become aware of the CURRENT

2.1 Identify a current ineffective behavior or habit you want to change. Write this behavior in the *CURRENT* textbox.

2.2 What were the negative outcomes or consequences of this behavior in the past? Write the negative outcomes on the *OUTCOMES* line.

2.3 What type of emotions do you experience when you behave this way? Write one-word emotions on the *EMOTIONS* line.

2.4 Which internal thoughts or external stimuli activate this behavior? Summarize your thoughts on the *ACTIVATION THOUGHTS* line.

2.5 Why do you behave this way? Indicate your reasons on the *REASONS* line.

Step 3: Become aware of the NEW

3.1 Think of a more effective habit or behavior. How would you describe this behavior in one sentence? Write a clear definition of this new behavior in the *NEW* textbox.

3.2 Why do you want to behave this way in future? List your reasons on the *REASONS* line.

3.3 What type of emotions will you experience in future when you adopt this new behavior? Write one-word emotions on the *EMOTIONS* line.

3.4 What impact will this behavior have on yourself and others? Write the outcomes on the *OUTCOMES* line.

3.5 Develop an implementation statement for yourself. ***If ... happens, I will do ... to achieve ...*** Write your activation sentence on the *ACTIVATION THOUGHTS* line.

Step 4: VISUALIZE success

4.1 Create a 'mental movie':
Visualize for 5 minutes on how you successfully adopt the new behavior, as indicated in the previous step, in a new situation. Emphasize images, sounds, and emotions in your mind.

4.2 Describe in one or two sentences what you visualized in the *VISUALIZE* textbox.

4.3 List the images, sounds, and emotions of your 'mental movie' in the textboxes provided.

4.4 Create a title (name) for your 'mental movie' and write it on top of the *VISUALIZATION* textbox.

Step 5: Take ACTION

5.1 List 1 to 3 practical actions you can implement in the next month to achieve your desired behavior.

WORK–LIFE SATISFACTION WHEEL

STEP 1:

Indicate on the graph below how satisfied you are in each area of your life (*0 = Highly dissatisfied; 10 = Highly satisfied*).

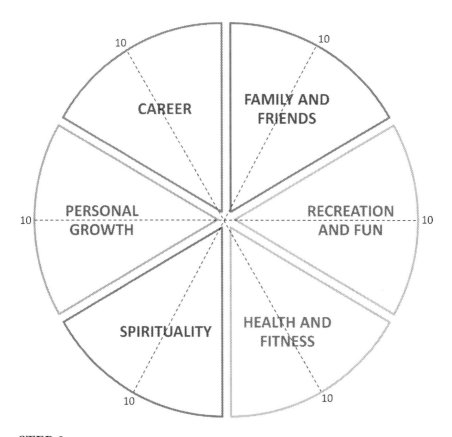

STEP 2:

List your score for each area in the table below.

Area	Score
A. Career	
B. Personal growth	
Intellectual health ((A+B) ÷ 2)	

C. Family and friends	
D. Recreation and fun	
Emotional health ((C+D) ÷ 2)	
E. Health and fitness	
Physical health (E)	
F. Spirituality	
Spiritual health (F)	

STEP 3:

Shade your score of each area in the graph below.

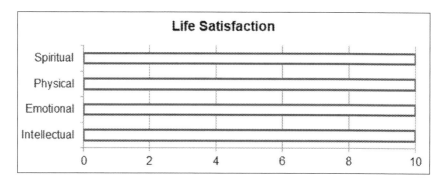

STEP 4:

Use the scores in step 2 to calculate personal work–life balance.

Energy takers (A + B + E) = ____ /30 x 100 = ____%
Energy givers (C + D + F) = ____/30 x 100 = ____%

PERSONAL CAREER PLAN GUIDE

Name:	
ID number:	
Date:	

PART 1: LIFE PURPOSE

Answer the following questions:

1.1 What is your life purpose? **(What)**
1.2 Why do you want to achieve this life purpose? **(Why)**
1.3 What knowledge (qualifications), skills (experience), abilities (natural talent), and attributes (personality characteristics and values) do you possess that could help you to achieve this life purpose? **(How)**

Use the answers to the above questions to compile a life purpose statement. The following sentence structure can be used as a guideline:

My purpose in life is to… (what) because… (why). I will achieve this purpose by applying my knowledge of…, my skills of…, my natural talent(s) of… and my attributes of…(how).

The values I live by are…

PART 2: CURRENT POSITION ALIGNMENT

Answer the following questions in terms of your current position:

1.1 On a scale of 1–10 (*1 = Poor alignment; 10 = Perfect alignment*), how well does your **life purpose** align with your current position? Indicate the score on the Alignment Wheel below.
1.2 On a scale of 1–10 (*1 = Poor alignment; 10 = Perfect alignment*), how well does your current **knowledge** (qualification) align with your current position? Indicate the score on the Alignment Wheel.
1.3 On a scale of 1–10 (*1 = Poor alignment; 10 = Perfect alignment*), how well do your current **skills** (experience) align with your current position? Indicate the score on the Alignment Wheel.

1.4 On a scale of 1–10 (*1 = Poor alignment; 10 = Perfect alignment*), how well do your current **abilities** (natural talents) align with your current position? Indicate the score on the Alignment Wheel.

1.5 On a scale of 1–10 (*1 = Poor alignment; 10 = Perfect alignment*), how well do your current **attributes** (personality and values) align with your current position? Indicate the score on the Alignment Wheel.

1.6 On a scale of 1–10 (*1 = Poor alignment; 10 = Perfect alignment*), how well does your life purpose align with the **organization's purpose**? Indicate the score on the Alignment Wheel.

ALIGNMENT WHEEL: CURRENT POSITION

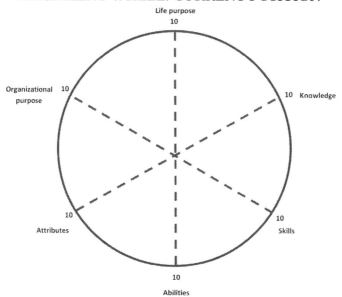

1.7 Review the completed Alignment Wheel and identify any alignment gaps.

PART 3: JOB CRAFTING

Answer the following question:

3 How can your life purpose, knowledge, skills, abilities, and attributes be better aligned to your current position?

Answer the following questions:

1.1 If anything is possible, what would your perfect future job be? Why?

1.2 What type of position or type of work would be your ideal future job?

Use the answers of 4.1 and 4.2 to note your ideal future position:

Use your **future ideal position** as basis and answer the following questions:

1.3 On a scale of 1–10 (*1 = Poor alignment; 10 = Perfect alignment*), how well does your **life purpose** align with the ideal position? Indicate the score on the Alignment Wheel below.

1.4 On a scale of 1–10 (*1 = Poor alignment; 10 = Perfect alignment*), how well does your current **knowledge** (qualifications) align with the ideal position? Indicate the score on the Alignment Wheel.

1.5 On a scale of 1–10 (*1 = Poor alignment; 10 = Perfect alignment*), how well do your current **skills** (experience) align with the ideal position? Indicate the score on the Alignment Wheel.

1.6 On a scale of 1–10 (*1 = Poor alignment; 10 = Perfect alignment*), how well do your current **abilities** (natural talents) align with the ideal position? Indicate the score on the Alignment Wheel.

1.7 On a scale of 1–10 (*1 = Poor alignment; 10 = Perfect alignment*), how well do your current **attributes** (personality and values) align with the ideal position? Indicate the score on the Alignment Wheel below.

1.8 On a scale of 1–10 (*1 = Poor alignment; 10 = Perfect alignment*), how well does the ideal position align with the **organization's purpose**? Indicate the score on the Alignment Wheel below.

ALIGNMENT WHEEL: FUTURE POSITION

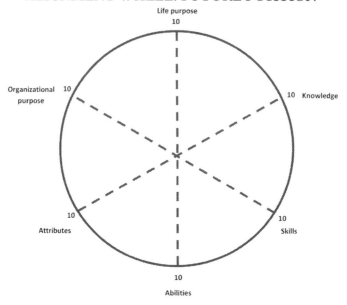

1.9 Review the completed Alignment Wheel and identify any gaps.

PART 5: CAREER PATH

Indicate in the spaces below your current, next, and future positions.

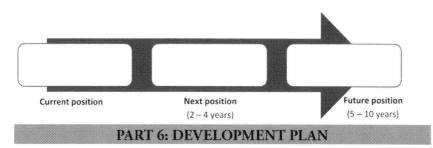

Current position | Next position (2 – 4 years) | Future position (5 – 10 years)

PART 6: DEVELOPMENT PLAN

Compile a Personal Development Plan (refer to the Personal Development Plan template) to:

- Close any gaps in the current alignment.
- Close any gaps in future alignment.
- Prepare yourself for the next and future position, in line with your life purpose.

PERSONAL DEVELOPMENT PLAN GUIDE

Name:
Position:
Date:

PART 1: CAREER PATH

Indicate your current, next, and future positions below per your Career Plan.

Current position   Next position   Future position
(2 – 4 years)   (5 – 10 years)

PART 2: COMPETENCE / ATTRIBUTE GAPS

Use the gaps identified in your Career Plan to complete the tables below.

Current positional gaps:
List your competency and attribute gaps in relation to your **current position** in the table below:

Dimension	Competence/ Attribute gap	Suggested learning activity (use Table 1, below, as a guide)	Learning type	Learning %
Knowledge		1. _____ 2. _____	Foundational	10%
Skills		1. _____ 2. _____	Experiential	70%
Abilities		1. _____ 2. _____		
Attributes		1. _____ 2. _____	Personal	20%

Future positional gaps:

List your competency and attribute gaps in relation to your **next position** in the table below:

Dimension	Competence/ Attribute gap	Suggested learning activity *(use Table 1, below, as a guide)*	Learning type	Learning %
Knowledge		1. _____ 2.	Foundational	10%
Skills		1. 2.	Experiential	70%
Abilities		1. 2.		
Attributes		1. _____ 2.	Personal	20%

Table 1. Types of Learning

Foundational learning	Experiential learning	Personal learning
Formal training (classroom)	On-the-job	Coaching
Electronic learning	Simulations	Mentoring
Seminars/Webinars	Gamification	Social learning
Conferences	Action learning	Reflection
Workshops	Workplace assignments	
Group learning		
Research		
Reading		
"learn-by-receiving"	"learn-by-doing"	"learn-by-transforming"
10%	70%	20%

PART 3: DEVELOPMENT PLAN

Use your answers in Step 2 and prioritize your top five learning activities in the table below. Also indicate a target date for each learning activity.

Priority	Learning course/Activity	Target date	Comment
1			
2			
3			
4			
5			

SELF-REFLECTION GUIDE

Answer the following questions:

What is the purpose of the self-reflection session?

What outcomes do you want to achieve from the self-reflection session?

Where will you self-reflect?

When will you self-reflect?

On which areas will you focus during the self-reflection session?

Use your answers to the previous questions to write a self-reflection intentional statement for your upcoming self-reflection session.

The purpose of the self-reflection session is to... At the end of the session, I want to have achieved the following outcomes... I will reflect at ... [place] on ... [date] from ... [start time] to ... [end time] and focus intensively on reflecting on the following areas ... [focus areas].

Step 1: Review the purpose and outcomes

Review the purpose and outcomes of the self-reflection session according to the self-reflection intention statement you compiled prior to the session

Step 2: Start reflecting on the focus areas

- Reflect intensively for 10 – 20 minutes on each focus area.
- Think about the inputs, reasons, actions, and outcomes of the focus area.
- Use the Thought Process Map when the focus area is behavior-related.
- Think about past events, current trends, and the future scenarios.
- Visualize success.

Step 3: Summarize your reflection thoughts in writing

- Make detailed written notes of your reflection.
- Summarize your reflection in one sentence.

Step 4: Evaluate the outcomes

- Evaluate the outcomes of the reflection session against the desired outcomes in your self-reflection intentional statement.

Step 5: Compile next steps

- Review your reflection summary.
- Determine the next steps.
- Prioritize your next steps by completing the table below.

Reflection area	Action	Due date	Measure of success

AFTER THE SELF-REFLECTION SESSION

Implement, measure, and review the planned action steps.

Plan your next self-reflection session.

CV-SCREENING SCORECARD (EXAMPLE)

JOB INFORMATION

Job title:	Civil Engineer
Occupational domain:	
Patterson band:	
Applicable division/department:	
Direct superior:	Project Manager

JOB REQUIREMENTS

EDUCATION / QUALIFICATIONS:

Type of qualification	Importance	Score		
		0	1	2
Qualification in Civil Engineering	Compulsory	No qualification	National Diploma	Degree
TOTAL SCORE				/2

OTHER REQUIREMENTS:

Type of requirement	Importance	Score	
		0	1
Professional registration	Compulsory	No	Yes
TOTAL SCORE			/1

EXPERIENCE:

Criteria	Importance	Score			
		1	2	3	4
Years' experience in a related role		0–2	3	4	5+
TOTAL SCORE					/4

Type of experience	Activities involved in	Importance	Score	
			0	1
SHEQ Management	• General SHEQ management • SHEQ Investigations • Behavior-based Safety • Risk Assessments	Compulsory	No	Yes
Financial Management	• General Financial Management • Risk Management	Compulsory	No	Yes

				/4
Construction Management	• Corporate Governance and Business Ethics • Risk Management • Sub-Contractors and Suppliers • Construction Project Planning • Project Management • Project Supervision • Construction QA/QC • Stores Management	Compulsory	No	Yes
Human Resource Management	• General Human Resource Management • Recruitment • Performance Management • Industrial Relations • Training and Development	Compulsory	No	Yes
TOTAL SCORE				

FINAL SCORES

Applicant	ID number	Final Score
		/11
		/11
		/11
		/11
		/11

COMPETENCY-BASED INTERVIEW GUIDE (EXAMPLE)

POSITION

Vacant Position: Executive HR Manager

APPLICANT DETAILS

Date of Interview:

INTERVIEWER

Name:
Position:

RATING SCALE

1	2	3	4	5
Poor	Less than acceptable	Acceptable	More than acceptable	Excellent

TIME FRAME

Opening	2 min
Key background review	5 min
Competency-based questions	15 min
General questions	15 min
Close	3 min
TOTAL	**45 min**

COMPETENCY-BASED QUESTIONS

Topic/Competency	Question	Comments	Score
Strategic HR management	What was your HR strategy in your previous role? How did you implement it and what was the result?		
HR risk management	How did you manage and mitigate HR-related risks in the past?		
HR optimization	Can you describe a time when you implemented new HR technology or best practices? What was the impact after implementation?		
HR infrastructure	In your view, what type of HR infrastructure is needed to execute an organizational strategy effectively?		
HR measurement	How did you track HR performance in the past? What type of HR measures did you use?		

Value creation	Can you share 1 or 2 examples of how you created value for multiple stakeholders in a previous HR Executive role?			
Work context	In your view, what are the major HR challenges and opportunities in the industry? What should a company do to overcome or pursue these?			
Leadership	Can you describe your leadership style or approach in one sentence? How was this approach effective in the past?			
TOTAL SCORE				

GENERAL QUESTIONS

Topic	Question	Comments	Score
TOTAL SCORE			

PANEL SCORES SUMMARY

Panel member				Total score

Total final	
Average final	

PSYCHOMETRIC ASSESSMENT BENCHMARK SCORECARD (EXAMPLE)

Position: Managing Director
Patterson Band:

Assessment Battery

Dimension	Test Instrument
Cognitive ability	Cognitive Processing Profile (CPP)
Personality	15 Factor Questionnaire Plus (15FQ+)
Derailing behavior	Hogan Development Survey (HDS)
Workplace risk behavior	Work-related risk and integrity scale (WRISc)
Emotional intelligence	Emotional Quotient Inventory (EQ-i 2.0)

Cognitive Ability

Dimension	Benchmark	Candidate (Yes = 1 / No = 0)
Preferred occupational domain (current)	Tactical strategy	
Preferred occupational domain (potential)	Parallel processing	
Preferred problem-solving styles	• Analytical • Integrative • Structured • Reflective	
Learning ability	High	
Score		/ 4

Personality

Personality trait	Benchmark	Candidate (Yes = 1 / No = 0)
Empathetic	Above average to high	
Accommodating	Above average	
Detail-orientated	High	
Self-confident	Above average to high	
Group orientated	Above average to high	
Self-disciplined	High	
Cope under pressure	High	
Score		/ 7

Derailed behavior

Behavioral tendency	Benchmark	Candidate (Low risk = 1 / Medium and high risk = 0)
Excitable	Low risk	
Skeptical	Low risk	
Cautious	Low risk	
Reserved	Low risk	
Leisurely	Low risk	
Bold	Low risk	
Mischievous	Low risk	
Colorful	Low risk	
Imaginative	Low risk	
Diligent	Low risk	
Dutiful	Low risk	
Score		/ 11

Workplace risk behavior

Risk behavior	Benchmark	Candidate (Low risk = 1 / Medium and high risk = 0)
Aggressive	Low risk	
Callous effect (uncaring)	Low risk	
Cynicism	Low risk	
Egotism	Low risk	
External locus of control	Low risk	
Impulsivity	Low risk	
Low effort control	Low risk	
Manipulative	Low risk	
Negative affect	Low risk	
Pessimism	Low risk	
Risk taking	Low risk	
Rule defiance	Low risk	
Score		/ 12

Emotional Intelligence

Risk behavior	Benchmark	Candidate (Yes = 1 / No = 0)
Self-perception	High	
Self-expression	High	

Interpersonal relationships	High	
Decision-making	High	
Stress management	High	
Score		**/ 4**

Final Scores

Name and Surname	ID number	Final score
		/ 38
		/ 38
		/ 38
		/ 38
		/ 38
		/ 38
		/ 38

VALUES FRAMEWORK (EXAMPLE)

The following is an example of an Organizational Values Framework:

Value statement	Behavior indicators	Value
Safely, we start and finish together	• Keep each employee safe and healthy • Provide a safe, healthy and effective work environment • Protect employees at all cost • Ensure zero fatalities	Safety
We drive excellence through ethical behavior	• Honest and trustworthy • Strong moral principles • Do business ethically • Stand up for what is right	Integrity
People matter because we care	• Kind and empathetic • Respect and understand others • Authentic care for employees	Compassion
We take ownership and consistently exceed expectations	• Deliver a quality product or service on time • Responsible and take ownership • High customer satisfaction	Delivery
We work together and embrace diversity to achieve greatness	• Work together as one team • Aim to achieve the same goals • Treat each other like family	Unity
With determination and focus we passionately strive towards excellence	• Loyal to the company • Dedicated and hard-working • Strive for excellence • Initiate continuous improvement	Commitment

ORGANIZATIONAL CREED (EXAMPLE)

The following is an example of an organizational creed:

The purpose of our business is to build sustainable infrastructure that ultimately uplifts society. As such, we build our nation by creating jobs, promoting socio-economic development, and bringing communities closer together.

Our vision is to become the preferred constructor, preferred employer, and preferred investment by delivering safe, profitable projects and services.

We achieve this by:

- Ensuring we start and finish each project together. Safety is an inherent part of everything we do. We care about the well-being of our employees, partners, communities, and the environment.
- Serving our clients and stakeholders with integrity. We have zero tolerance for unethical behavior or business practices.
- Cultivating Ubuntu, because people matter. We are responsible for ensuring everyone is valued and respected, regardless of race, gender, or culture.
- Taking ownership and consistently exceeding expectations to deliver high-quality projects.
- Working together, embracing diversity, and aiming to achieve a common objective.
- Striving towards excellence. We are passionate, focused, determined, loyal, and dedicated. We expand our boundaries by continuously improving the way we do things to add value for our employees, customers, and shareholders.

Using the values of safety, integrity, compassion, delivery, unity, and commitment as our foundation, we are committed to building a legacy and remaining a sustainable business for future generations.

LEADER–EMPLOYEE DIAGNOSTIC FORM

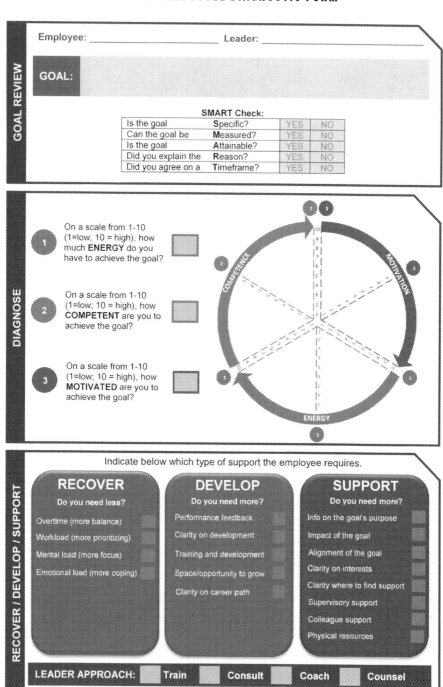

Employee: _____ Leader: _____

GOAL REVIEW

GOAL:

SMART Check:

Is the goal	Specific?	YES	NO
Can the goal be	Measured?	YES	NO
Is the goal	Attainable?	YES	NO
Did you explain the	Reason?	YES	NO
Did you agree on a	Timeframe?	YES	NO

DIAGNOSE

1. On a scale from 1-10 (1=low; 10 = high), how much **ENERGY** do you have to achieve the goal?

2. On a scale from 1-10 (1=low; 10 = high), how **COMPETENT** are you to achieve the goal?

3. On a scale from 1-10 (1=low; 10 = high), how **MOTIVATED** are you to achieve the goal?

COMPETENCE MOTIVATION ENERGY

RECOVER / DEVELOP / SUPPORT

Indicate below which type of support the employee requires.

RECOVER	**DEVELOP**	**SUPPORT**
Do you need less?	Do you need more?	Do you need more?
Overtime (more balance)	Performance feedback	Info on the goal's purpose
Workload (more prioritizing)	Clarity on development	Impact of the goal
Mental load (more focus)	Training and development	Alignment of the goal
Emotional load (more coping)	Space/opportunity to grow	Clarity on interests
	Clarity on career path	Clarity where to find support
		Supervisory support
		Colleague support
		Physical resources

LEADER APPROACH: ☐ Train ☐ Consult ☐ Coach ☐ Counsel

LEADER APPROACH GUIDE (TRAIN)

LEADER APPROACH | TRAIN | CONSULT | COACH | COUNSEL

WHAT?

1. **Clarify the goal**
   - The goal we want to achieve is ...

2. **Provide constructive feedback**
   - The things you did well so far in relation to this goal were ...
   - The things you need to do more of are ...
   - I think your current strengths of ... can be useful to achieve this goal. I want you to use these more.

3. **Discuss competence gaps**
   - You mentioned in the diagnostic session that you still need guidance on how to complete this goal. In which areas do you need help?
   - In my observation, it seems that you could benefit from ... training. Do you agree?

HOW?

1. **Provide solutions**
   - You mentioned that you still need help with ..., right? Let me show you exactly how to do this.
   - What could help in addition is to consult with the following persons ...
   - The following training courses might also help ...
   - The following books, articles, or website could also be helpful ...
   - Let's schedule a weekly mentoring session. You can use this session to ask any questions or to sound-board ideas. How does that sound?

2. **Confirm needs**
   - Is there anything else I can do to help you become more skillful in this area?

WHEN?

1. **Partner on target dates**
   - Which dates will be convenient for the weekly mentoring sessions?
   - Which dates will be convenient for the training?
   - Can I help you set up meetings with the following persons ...?
   - Can we agree to achieve this goal by ...?

LEADER APPROACH GUIDE (CONSULT)

LEADER APPROACH | TRAIN | **CONSULT** | COACH | COUNSEL

WHAT?

1. **Clarify the goal**
   - The goal we want to achieve is ...

2. **Identify the problem**
   - It seems that you are a bit overwhelmed by this goal. What are some of the current barriers or limitations (things that makes it difficult for you to complete this goal)?
   - I also observed the following barriers and limitations ... It seems that you need more guidance on how to... Is that right?

3. **Identify reasons**
   - In my view, possible reasons for the problem might be ... What is your view?
   - It seems that the following factors are draining your energy... Do you agree?

HOW?

1. **Provide solutions**
   - From what we said, I think the following will be a good action plan to resolve these problems...
   - Let's prioritize the work to be done. The most important thing to do is ..., then ..., etc.
   - I suggest you focus on completing only one thing at a time. Focus on completing ... before you start with ... Thereafter do ...
   - You mentioned you still need help with ..., right? Let's schedule a weekly mentoring session in which you can ask questions or sound-board ideas. How does that sound?
   - May I suggest that you take regular small breaks during the day? Also ensure you get enough rest after a work day. This might help increase your energy levels.
   - Maybe some time off with family and friends will help you to recover your energy levels. When was the last time you took leave?

2. **Confirm needs**
   - Is there anything else I can do to help you cope with the work demands?
   - Is there anything else I can do to help you become more skilful in any area?

WHEN?

1. **Partner on target dates**
   - Let's set dates for the Action Plan items. By when do you want to complete Item 1, Item 2, etc.?
   - Can we agree on the following short breaks during your work day?
   - If you need some time off, when would you want to take leave?
   - Can we agree to achieve this goal by ...?

LEADER APPROACH GUIDE (COACH)

LEADER APPROACH | TRAIN | CONSULT | **COACH** | COUNSEL

WHAT?

1. **Ask goal**
   - What is the goal you want to achieve?

2. **Ask purpose**
   - Why is this goal important to you?
   - Imagine you achieved this goal, what impact will it have on yourself, others, and the company?
   - How does this goal support your life's purpose?
   - How does this goal support the company's vision, mission, and strategy?

3. **Ask achievement**
   - Which positive milestones did you achieve thus far in relation to this goal?
   - What kind of emotions comes to mind when you think of these achievements?

HOW?

1. **Ask solutions**
   - What can you do in the next week to get closer to this goal?
   - What can you do differently to achieve this goal?
   - What else can you do?
   - Will it be all right if we prioritize your listed actions? Which action do you want to do first?

2. **Ask needs**
   - Is there anything I can do to help or support you to achieve this goal?

WHEN?

1. **Partner on target dates**
   - By when do you want to complete action 1 ..., action 2 ..., etc.?
   - By when do you want to achieve this goal?

LEADER APPROACH GUIDE (COUNSEL)

LEADER APPROACH | TRAIN | CONSULT | COACH | **COUNSEL**

WHAT?

1. Ask goal
- What is the goal you want to achieve?

2. Ask problem
- What are some of the barriers or limitations you experience in relation to this goal?
- What are some of the things that drain your energy?

3. Ask purpose
- Imagine you achieved this goal, what impact will it have on yourself, others, and the company?
- How does this goal support your life's purpose?
- How does this goal support the company's vision, mission, and strategy?

HOW?

1. Ask solutions
- What can you do to overcome the listed barriers or limitations?
- What can you do to recover your energy levels?
- How can you prioritize or organize your work better?
- What can you do to regain your focus?
- What can you do differently to achieve this goal?

2. Ask needs
- Is there anything I can do to help or support you to achieve this goal?

WHEN?

1. Partner on target dates
- Will it be all right if we put all your actions in an action plan with completion dates?
- By when do you want to achieve this goal?

About the Author

Dr. Michiel F. Coetzer is a qualified industrial and organizational psychologist and Neuroleadership coach. He has more than 14 years' experience in organizational development, leadership development, human resources management, learning and development, and coaching. He is the Managing Director and Founder of a research and development company named Wisdomy and a part-time lecturer at the University of Stellenbosch Business School for Executive Development. Dr. Coetzer was previously the Head of Organizational Effectiveness and the acting HR Executive at an international construction company, mainly responsible to enhance people, organizational, and leadership effectiveness in the Group. He was also a Director and Co-owner of a national furniture manufacturer and retailer, earlier in his career, looking after business development and human resource management.

Dr. Coetzer holds a Ph.D. in leadership and a Master's degree (M.com) in industrial and organizational psychology. He also completed a brain-based coaching certificate with the Neuroleadership Institute, a counseling diploma, and several psychometric accreditation courses.

Dr. Coetzer presented several papers at national and international conferences and published articles in various scientific and non-scientific journals.

Printed in the United States
By Bookmasters